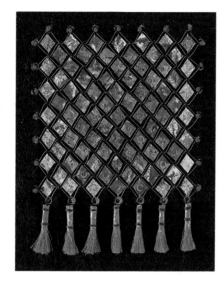

The Art and Craft of Appliqué

The Art and Craft of
Appliqué

Juliet **B**awden

GROVE WEIDENFELD
NEW YORK

For Mike, Jack, Oliver, Jessica and Alice

Edited and designed by Mitchell Beazley
International Ltd.
Artists House, 14-15 Manette Street,
London W1V 5LB

Art Editor **Larraine Lacey**
Editor **Victoria Davenport**
Editorial Assistant **Rachel Addis**
Typesetter **Kerri Hinchon**
Production **Ted Timberlake**
Senior Executive Art Editor **Jacqui Small**
Executive Editor **Judith More**

Photography **Peter Marshall**
Illustrations **Kevin Hart**

Published by Grove Weidenfeld
A division of Grove Press, Inc.
841 Broadway
New York, NY 10003-4793

Library of Congress Cataloging-in-Publication Data

Bawden, Juliet.
    The art and craft of appliqué / Juliet Bawden.
        p.   cm.
    ISBN 0-8021-1455-5 : $24.95
    1. Appliqué.   I. Title
TT779.B39 1991   91-16684
746.44'5–dc20   CIP

The publishers have made every effort to ensure
that all instructions given in this book are accurate and
safe, but they cannot accept liability for any resulting
injury, damage or loss to either person or property
whether direct or consequential and howsoever arising.
The author and publishers will be grateful for any
information which will assist them in keeping future
editions up to date.

Typeset in Gill and Perpetua
Colour reproduction by Scantrans Pte Ltd, Singapore
Printed in Spain by Graficas Estella, S.A., Navarra

10 9 8 7 6 5 4 3 2 1

Contents

foreword

I have had a passion for textiles for as long as I can remember, which I probably inherited from my Armenian mother. Some of my earliest memories are of watching her making clothes for the family and then acquiring the fabric scraps for my own creations. At an early age she showed me how to make lace. Brought up in an orphanage, as a child her most coveted possession was a needle.

My love of fabrics, colour and texture led me to study textiles at art school. The excitement of being able to create, embellish and decorate fabrics in many different ways has never left me. This irresistible urge to create drives many of the appliqué artists you will find in this book. They come from many different backgrounds – some are art-school-trained, others are self-taught or have taken up appliqué through adult education classes.

The book is divided into sections, starting with a short guide to some historical and folk art aspects of this international craft, followed by sections on some of the traditional methods of working in appliqué. The majority of the book covers work made by current practitioners and shows you how to create your own appliqués. The book is designed as an inspirational tool which will set you on the road to creating your own works. There are sections on art, fashion, soft furnishings and three-dimensional appliqué.

I would like to say thank you to all the artists who generously contributed work to be photographed in this book. A full list of contributors is given with other acknowledgments on pages 138 and 144.

Left: Two simple appliqués constructed from hand-rolled felt. The vase on the far left was inlaid (see p.34) into the background, then decorated with felt and netting flowers and leaves which were stuck in place with glue. The picture is finished with random lines of machine stitching. The appliqué near left was made by gluing felt flowers and leaves onto a background made up of strips of brightly coloured felts woven into a piece of pale felt. (Liz Mundle)

perspectives

Right: A collection of American appliqué quilts, circa 1850. The example in the top right-hand corner is an unusual cot quilt, while the quilt shown in the lower right hand corner makes use of small print fabrics to produce a flower basket design; each basket contains a different motif, such as a bunch of flowers or a group of birds. (Susan Jenkins)

The following pages look at some of the historical aspects of appliqué worldwide. Even before fabrics were woven, people embellished matted cloths, such as felt, beaten bark or leather skins, with applied decorations as diverse as fish scales, leaves, beads or even birds' feathers.

Although appliqué is known to have been made from earliest times, very little remains because fabric, unlike pottery, is easily destroyed by everyday wear and tear, and by sunlight. The most ancient piece of applied work still in existence dates from about 980 BC. Believed to be a ceremonial canopy, it is made of dyed gazelle hide that has been cut into the many different patterns used in the cartouches and symbols of ancient Egypt.

Felt appliqué was practised by the nomadic cattle-breeding tribes of the Gobi Desert as early as 200 BC; appliquéd saddle-covers and a wall-hanging have been found in Siberian tombs.

Beautiful hangings decorated with plants, animals, birds, portraits and dancing figures, dating from AD 300 to 1000, have been found in Egyptian burial sites. As in India, animals were revered in Egypt, which resulted in many of them being buried in the royal tombs of the pharaohs. When the animals were discovered during excavations, they were found wrapped in decorative appliqués. A linen collar with appliquéd petals was found in the 3,000-year-old tomb of Tutankhamen. During this time the Copts of Egypt are also known to have decorated their plain robes with woven roundels, squares, stripes and L-shaped corners.

During the Middle Ages, throughout Europe appliqué could be found on household furnishings. It was also used for banners and for military and ecclesiastical clothing; for example, the Crusaders wore surcoats on which emblems were embroidered or applied. Because textiles were scarce and thus expensive, appliqué developed as a way of reusing pieces of rich and rare woven fabrics that were too precious to throw away. Embroidery silks were costly, so fragments of valuable cloth were used as a substitute for embroidery. The first reference to a quilt believed to include appliqué is in a French book of 12th- and 13th-century love poems, where one poem refers to a quilt decorated with a border of appliqué flowers.

America

The strong tradition of quilted, patchwork and appliqué quilts in America was in part due to the Navigation Acts of 1651 and 1660, which were passed to protect England's trade monopolies, particularly in textiles. With the passing of the Acts, which were in force until 1826, it became illegal for the colonists to manufacture textiles, or to buy them from any country but England. It was during this time that the pieced quilt was born. One of the earliest forms of patchwork piecing was the crazy quilt, which

consisted of random pieces of fabric covering a ground cloth. It arose as a way of recycling the good parts of worn clothes and bedclothes.

Despite these laws, some textile machinery was smuggled into America and American cotton then exported to England. This met with howls of protest from British wool and flax traders, which led in turn to the importation of cotton being declared illegal in Britain; by 1729 it even was illegal to wear cotton in America. However, by 1736 the laws were being so flouted that they had to be repealed. Instead, heavy taxes were imposed on the colonists. Meanwhile, the British were also having problems with the import-ation of brilliantly painted, printed and embroidered cottons from the Indies. Despite efforts to suppress importation, many of these textiles were smuggled into England and America. The strong decorative effects of even small pieces of these new materials, and the desire to make the most of them, probably prompted their use in pieced and appliqué techniques, and thus the popularity of these quilts. As well, the quilts gave a kind of "instant" embroidery, in that whole images of animals, plants and people could be cut out and then stitched down.

In the 1840s a new fashion appeared, known as the album quilt. Constructed of blocks, usually appliquéd, the album quilt was made by a group of women, friends or relatives of the person to whom the finished quilt was given. Each block – like an album page – presented the recipient with a verse or picture along with a signature by which its maker could be remembered. The most outstanding examples are the elaborate Baltimore album quilts, which were constructed using the broderie perse method, some-times known as cretonne appliqué.

Initially, the use of chintzes in appliqué quilts was not particularly creative; flowers and petals cut from the fabric remained as they were, applied to a white background. However, as the art of appliqué grew, so did its subject matter, and its construction became more imaginative. For example, in a quilt called "The Trade and Commerce Bedcover", made in 1830 by Hannah Stockton of New Jersey, the use of fabric is very free, with sail boats of floral chintz and a tartan rowing boat.

Appliqué shows us not only the materials available, but also the everyday pursuits, politics and fashions of that time. The two great social reform movements in America during the 19th century were temperance and the abolition of slavery, and quilts often were made as a means of fund-raising and moral persuasion. People who contributed to the cause had their names embroidered on the quilts, which were then raffled to make money.

The United Kingdom

The Elizabethan Age was one of the great ages of English embroidery. During this time there was a prodigious output of domestic needlework, including bed-curtains, valances and coverlets, worked with embroidery and appliqué. Hangings covered in appliqué decorated the palaces, castles and houses of Tudor Britain. Some of the most exciting are the 16th-century wall-hangings in Hardwick Hall in Derbyshire, England, worked by the Countess of Shrewsbury, "Bess of Hardwick".

Following the founding of the East India Company, chintz began to arrive in London in small quantities. The colours of these chintzes were much brighter than anything available in Europe. In 1643 a director of the Company requested a change from the indigenous Indian designs they had been producing. Indian chintzes printed with chinoiserie ornamentation for the English market were often used in appliqué work.

The growth of the printed textile industry in Britain was spurred on by the popularity of Indian imports. At the beginning of the 19th century, designs were based on Indian, Egyptian, and Chinese themes; these gave way to a new trend based on pastoral scenes, game birds, and classical architecture. In 1830 one Carlisle printer began to produce textiles depicting important buildings like Euston Station in London. These large-scale motifs were particularly appropriate for the broderie perse technique. Also during the early part of the 19th century the vogue for printed medallions and borders, often referred to as Sheraton panels, began. These panels were ideal for quilt-makers, who could simply appliqué them into the middle of their work.

At the same time, paper-cutting became part of quilt design. The cut-out was usually in Turkey red appliquéd onto a white background and sometimes the red cut-outs were designed so that they simulated block quilts.

The most exciting development of appliqué in the 19th century is known as inlay work, which resembles marquetry and cloisonné enamel, with each piece outlined in chain-stitch or gold couching. Inlay work required a great deal of skill and patience; the fabric pieces had to butt each other, and the cloth had to be thick enough to hold the oversewing, which was done from the back with very tiny stitches, while the construction was taking place. Embroidery stitches, which were purely decorative, were added later. The work was used mainly to produce pictures in cloth. Many popular and historical prints were reproduced by this method.

As appliqué grew in popularity, the designs became excessive and vulgar. Yet however tasteless these quilts may be, they provide us with a social record of the times as they often included cut-outs

Right: A collection of hand appliquéd table linen produced in China in the 1920s and 1930s, some for home use, much for export.

This style was popular in Britain during the 1930s and patterns were printed in books and magazines for needlewomen to copy.

appliquéd into place of fashionable apparel such as top-hats and fans, as well as domestic trivia like candlesticks, cups, even household pets.

Toward the end of the 19th century there was a reaction to this richness of colour and overwhelming pattern. The Royal School of Needlework, established in 1876, aimed to restore ornamental needlework to the place it formerly had held in the decorative arts. The success of the School launched "art needlework" as a movement, and books began to be published on the new methods of design and application.

The Arts and Crafts Movement also influenced needlework; it heralded the end of the rich Victorian work and changed people's attitudes toward colour, fabric and design, bringing about a desire for simplicity. Concurrent with the Arts and Crafts Movement was the work being done at the Glasgow School of Art by Jessie Rowat Newbery and her pupil Ann Macbeth. Jessie Rowat's needlework, which included appliqué, was original in all aspects; she encouraged new colour schemes – grays, silvers and lilacs, as well as black and white – and stressed that complicated stitches were not necessarily the criterion of fine embroidery.

Much 19th century appliqué work was produced for domestic use and appliqué continued to be used to decorate household items, such as tray . cloths, dishtowels and runners, well into the 1930s. Recently

Left: These 1930s appliqué quilts are American in origin. The quilt in the top left hand corner has a large central tree of life motif while the quilt below it is made up of individual pictorial motifs. The other two quilts, although appliqué, are more like pieced quilts with their even patterns. The soft green, rose and white colour scheme was especially popular at the time that they were made.

it has had a revival, more as an art form than for domestic use. A major piece of work, designed by Sandra Lawrence, and carried out by 20 ladies of the Royal School of Needlework, is the Overlord Embroidery. Completed in 1973, it tells the story of the Normandy Landings, D-Day, 6th June 1944.

France

Appliqué was particularly popular in the 19th century; the method used was an ancient technique known as *broderie-appliqué* which had been practised as far back as the Middle Ages. The fabrics were first glued onto thin paper, then this paper/fabric sandwich was put in a press to remove air bubbles. Next, the pattern was drawn onto the back of the paper and the pieces were cut out. Finally, the pieces were glued onto the background fabric and sewn into position (either using piping or satin stitch to cover and finish the edges).

Asia

India In the 18th and 19th centuries, leather appliqué was practised by the Mochis of Kutch, part of Gujarat, who learned their skills from Muslim craftsmen at the end of the 16th and beginning of the 17th centuries. The leathers were coloured in black, red and green, and embroidered with silver and gold chain-stitch. In Kutch and Sind, leather appliqué was also used to cover shields.

Japan Japanese embroidery has Chinese and Korean origins and was practised from as far back as the 6th century. Although appliqué (*Kittsuke*) was frequently used in high class works, it was not used to the extent that it was in the medieval and later European embroideries. Figures worked in gold and silver threads were stitched to a ground and moulded in relief over padding.

Azerbaijan Most Azerbaijani embroidery, including appliqué, features geometric patterning taken from architectural masterpieces of the 18th century. Appliqué was particularly popular during the 18th and 19th centuries for the decoration of prayer rugs.

The Far North

Because appliqué with inlaying and padding can add warmth to garments, it is often used in countries with cooler climates. Both the Inuits of Greenland and the Lapps of northern Scandinavia used the fur and skin of caribou, reindeer and seals, as well as fish skins and wools, in their appliquéd garments.

Siberia An unusual form of appliqué was practised in Siberia; that of hair embroidery. Strands of reindeer hair were laid and couched with sinew thread as part of an appliquéd skin composition. This form of appliqué was also practised by North American Indians - hardly surprising given that the Bering Strait separates Asia from North America at its narrowest point by only 36 miles.

Russia

Much Russian embroidery, including appliqué, is religious. By the beginning of the 18th century, Russia imported damasks from Broussa, Anatolia (Turkey) and Arabia, taffeta from France and satin from China, Turkey, Afghanistan, Persia and Venice. With these raw materials came new designs and methods of embroidery. However, although much embroidery is found from this time, little of it is appliqué work except for decoration in the form of sewn-on jewels and metal plaques.

One documented use of appliqué in the 18th century is the costume of the Kremlin guard, who wore deep rose velvet coats which featured an applied emblem of a two-headed eagle with a central motif of George slaying the dragon.

It is in the late 19th and early 20th centuries that appliqué came into its own as an element of new Russian art forms, especially in theatrical design. In 1909 the Russian impresario Sergei Diaghilev took Paris by storm with his production of the ballet "Scheherazade". The exotic appliquéd costumes, designed by Leon Bakst, brought a new wave of orientalism into fashion and the decorative arts.

folk **a**rt **t**raditions

Appliqué has been, and still is, carried out in many rural and industrialized communities, following traditional styles that have not changed for centuries. In some countries the work is done to sustain an ever-hungry tourist trade; in others, such as Chile, it is a way of making political statements.

India and Pakistan

In India, where labour and materials are cheap, traditional techniques and patterns are used in the fashion industry. Garments are often hand-appliquéd, and then sold to Western countries.

Appliqués used to be made by poor farming people, who often would recycle old fabrics. The better appliqués were, and still are, used to decorate large festivals, for example religious gatherings and wedding days. Because animals such as camels and bullocks are revered, they are often covered in heraldic-looking appliqué.

The Jaisalmer region has a tradition of outstandingly beautiful embroidery. Here, the women decorate almost everything they can with embroidered fabric; appliqué consists of geometric patterns worked in dark, earthy colours.

The *pichwai* of Nathdwara, Rajasthan is an embroidered cloth-hanging used as a decoration in

Above: The figures in this Peruvian appliqué were individually made and hand-sewn into position. Note the use of large feather and blanket embroidery stitches to finish off motifs and the large blanket stitch border that frames the design.

Right: A colourful **arpillera,** *depicting rural life in Peru. The fruit on the tree is padded, as are the lambs, giving an extra dimension to the composition. Texture is exploited too; the lambs are in a fleecy fabric. (Oxfam Trading)*

Hindu temples, which depicts the god Srinathji, with his dark-blue face, surrounded by milkmaids. Although traditionally embroidered, *pichwais* are also appliquéd.

Gujarat has its own distinctive style of appliqué, based on patchwork, in which pieces of coloured and patterned fabric are cut finely in different sizes, shapes and colours and sewn onto a plain background. Gujarat appliqué is used only on household items, which are often brilliantly coloured and highly ornamented with motifs such as peacocks, horse riders and elephants.

Khatwa is the name given to the appliqué work of Bihar. It is used on tents and canopies for ceremonial occasions. The designs are usually Persian-style trees, flowers, animals and birds.

Afghanistan

Here, garments are decorated with appliqué which takes the form of round cotton patches known as *guls,* onto which tiny beads are sewn in rosette patterns until the *gul* is completely covered. The *guls* are sewn onto embroideries into which little round mirrors are incorporated. The result is an extremely rich-looking clothing fabric.

Thailand

In the hills of Thailand live the Hmong, whose women wear indigo-dyed garments, the borders and panels of which are appliquéd with geometric motifs in red, yellow and black, often decorated with laid and couched work. In Bangkok the appliqué is completely different, with bold lions and dragons edged in chain, running and buttonhole stitch.

Tibet

Buddhist temples in Tibet were decorated with appliquéd hangings known as *tankas,* which usually had a central figure of a god or a saint. Traditionally, Tibetan appliqués were made from silk, wool or cotton; they were used for wall-hangings, tent panels, clothing and saddle-bags. The images depicted were mythological creatures, such as dragons.

Iran

The Resht region of İran is famous for a particular style of inlaid appliqué. Wall-hangings depicting flora are made from felt, cotton or wool. The applied pieces were held in position with tambour-work (continuous lines of chain stitch worked in a frame with a tambour hook) and embellished with seed pearls and gold and silver thread couched with silk.

North American Indians

Traditionally, Inuit appliqué was used to decorate clothing from indigenous materials such as seal skin. Today, the appliqués take the form of wall-hangings, made for sale, that reflect the activities of the Inuit, such as hunting and fishing.

American Indian women have adapted totem motifs, originally used in body-painting, to their weaving and applied fabric designs. Strong hard-wearing fabrics such as canvas and leather are used to make items such as moccasins or pouches, which are often decorated with appliquéd fringes, laces, shells and beads.

The Hawaiian Islands

A century after Captain Cook discovered the Polynesian archipelago, English missionaries were teaching patchwork to the local women. When the patches the missionaries brought with them ran out, the Hawaiians, who had taken to the technique, cut their patches from new cloth, and Hawaiian appliqué was born.

The motifs are large and intricate – and often the size of a full-scale quilt. The shapes on the quilts are inspired by natural forms such as figs, pineapples and forget-me-nots. The motifs are symbolic and are used again and again in different combinations. Traditionally, the different patterns were associated with particular families and therefore copying a pattern was frowned upon.

Hawaiian quilts are made in reverse quilting. The white, top, fabric is folded and the shape is cut out; then the fabric piece that retains the outline is hem-stitched to the brighter background colour so that the brightly coloured motif appears as a second layer of fabric. Original colours were vivid red on a white background. Later green appeared, and, later still, the Hawaiian royal colours of red and bright yellow became popular.

Central and South America

The important textile traditions of Central and South America involved primarily the decoration of clothing. This colourful, elaborate embroidery work is thought to have a long history.

Mexico Although textile traditions of weaving, dyeing and embroidery are strong in Mexico, appliqué is only practised in the form of embellishment using ribbons, braid, tassels and lace.

Panama The art of the *mola* ("blouse") is unique to Panama, particularly the San Blas Islands. Before the invasion of French colonists, the native Kunas "dressed" by painting their bodies. When they began to wear clothing in the mid-1800s, the Kunas simply transferred the designs to their clothes.

Molas are a very distinctive style of appliqué, being made of two or more layers of fabric that are cut through to reveal different colours, creating a contour

Previous page: These Indian tablecloths and wall-hangings each use a restricted colour palette and simple shapes, which are repeated as if they were printed with a wood block. The motifs are finished with bold embroidery stitches that highlight the simple, colourful shapes. (Neal Street East)

Right: These Indian hand-sewn cushion or pillow covers are worked using a reverse appliqué technique (see p. 38) in silks and cottons. The colour schemes – whites on beige and pinks with cream – show that these items were made for export to the West. (General Trading Company)

effect. The oldest *molas* usually have three layers of black, red and yellow. The designs were either stylized human, animal or floral forms.

Peru In recent years, an appliquéd hanging known as an *arpillera* has become a source of income for poor Peruvian women. The technique, which originated in Chile, often depicts scenes from everyday life with a mass of detail (for example, washing hanging on the line or vegetables on sale in the market).

Chile Chilean appliqués are bright in colour and naive in form. They usually carry a strong political statement. The images reflect the lives of the people in their impoverished shanty towns.

Africa

Where appliqué is found in Africa, it usually is associated with prestige and social position – for example the banners and flags which at one time proliferated in some parts of the continent.

The best-documented West African banners are those produced by the Fon people of Dahomey, now the republic of Benin. A restricted guild in Abomey produced the appliqué work, which included ceremonial caps and state umbrellas, as well as flags and banners.

The Sudan also produced flags and banners, as well as a distinctive appliquéd uniform, the *jibbeh*. Among the Kuba of Zaire the women wear a long, voluminous appliquéd cloth, which is wound around their waist, while in East and South Africa, applied work takes the form of bead decoration.

Central Europe

Although little appliqué work exists as part of contemporary folk art, in the past various European countries and regions have had strong traditions of appliqué. For example, the most precious item of a Hungarian woman's costume was a waistcoat made of sheepskin and decorated with appliqué patches, known as a *kodmon*. While in Romania garments such as shirts, waistcoats and jackets were decorated with appliqué designs.

Left: These African appliqué lengths, from 19th century Zaire, were wound around the body to form skirts. Self-appliqué, where both the ground and the motif fabric are the same and the contrast is achieved from the colour of the thread, is a simple technique that produces a sophisticated result. A solid overcast stitch and a crisp raffia cloth enhances the geometric pattern. (Paul Hughes)

Right: A collection of Ghanaian appliqué flags and banners, dating from 19th-century colonial Africa. The images and stitching used are naive in style. (Paul Hughes)

design **i**deas

Appliqué design can be inspired by many things – textures, colours and patterns of fabrics, or particular themes, or a combination of the two. Museums are full of visual references, and art galleries, antique shops, fruit and vegetable markets, parks or gardens can all be starting points for a design. Books and other printed matter also provide sources of inspiration for both colour and pattern. You may want to carry a sketchbook or camera with you so that you can compile a visual record of such references.

The individual approach to design differs greatly from artist to artist; some make a plan and stick rigidly to it, others work and rework designs until they are satisfied with the result. And appliqué artists create their designs in very different ways. Some work directly with fabric and scissors, cutting shapes and moving them about until a balanced composition is achieved. Others use paper pattern pieces which they then draw around with tailor's chalk, marking the position of each shape so that the fabric can be pinned into place. The advantage of working with paper pattern pieces is that if you wish to enlarge or reduce a design, or make repeats, you can use a photo-copying machine, and no fabric is wasted.

If you have a Polaroid camera, an interesting method of working is to place the design elements in position and then photograph them. If you are not happy with the photograph of the design, you can re-arrange the pieces and take another.

Left: Two rich machine appliqué pieces inspired by architectural details. The clever use of machine stitching helps to form perspective. Depth is conveyed by layering fabrics and using haberdashery. (Faith Manzira)

Above: Some of the best ideas for appliqué pieces come from your everyday surroundings. The artist has used a mixture of techniques; as well as appliqué, dyeing, printing and machine embroidery also feature. (Sandra Francis)

materials and equipment

Sewing equipment

○ *Tape measure, metre rule or yardstick*
○ *Tailor's chalk*
○ *Standard and embroidery needles*
○ *Steel or brass pins*
○ *Dressmaker's ruler*
○ *Magnet (for pins)*
○ *Wrist-held pin-cushion*
○ *Thimble*
○ *Dressmaking and embroidery scissors*
○ *Pinking shears*
○ *Cotton thread in standard and quilting strength*
○ *Basting (tacking) thread*
○ *Sewing machine with embroidery function*

One of the advantages of appliqué as a craft is that most of the materials and equipment that are needed can be found in your own home. The basic requirements are just a needle, thread and fabric.

Start a collection of fabrics that covers a range of colours, patterns, textures and thicknesses. You should include cotton, silk and wool fabrics. Cotton is available in many weights and textures, it is easy to cut, holds folds well, doesn't change shape and frays very little. Silk is useful because it has a suppleness that allows it to drape beautifully, a lustre that gives it a jewel-like appearance and when dyed the colours are rich. The structure of woollen fibres allows them to hold air, which gives wool its elasticity. Many tweeds, with their characteristic subtle mix of earthy and warm tones, are made from wool. These may be put to good use as parts of a landscape – for example tree trunks, rocks and cliffs. You can also use tweed to represent foodstuffs such as bread or biscuits.

When choosing patterns, take into account the scale on which you are working: while small motifs are versatile, large ones have a limited number of uses. Bear in mind that some fabrics fray more easily than

others and may be difficult to work with. Because it doesn't fray, and so there is no need to hem, felt is an ideal fabric for appliqué. Texture and sheen should be considered, too. On a single piece of work you can use two pieces of the same velvet and by changing the direction of the nap you can achieve two completely different tones. This can help create an illusion of depth. Corduroy comes in many thicknesses of rib and is a good fabric to use when you wish to direct the eye toward a particular area or object. It is especially effective in landscapes to suggest furrowed fields. And satin is suitable for anything which needs a sheen such as water, glossy paintwork, jewelry or wet pavements.

How you plan to use the appliqué will have some bearing on the fabrics you select. For example, appliqué on a garment which will be worn frequently is best worked in machine-washable fabrics that will not shrink, stretch or shed dye. It is a good rule of thumb to wash and iron fabric before you use it, to remove any "finish".

It is useful to store your fabrics in separate bags by pattern, texture and colour.

General equipment

○ *Iron, ironing board and pressing cloth*
○ *Latex-based glue*
○ *Sketchbook, pencils and pens*
○ *Sharp craft knife*
○ *Camera (for recording things of interest)*
○ *Tracing paper*
○ *Iron-on glue-impregnated gauze or interfacing*
○ *Fuse or florist's wire*
○ *Ruler and set square*
○ *Fabric paint*
○ *Coloured pencils*

Right: A broad selection of materials can be used for appliqué.
(Maureen Sawyer)

TECHNIQUES

before you **b**egin

Right: This landscape,
in acid-dyed, carded
fleece overlaid with
cottons and silks, was
inspired by the artist's
travel sketchbooks.
(Jeanette Appleton)

Previous page: Dyeing,
batik, overlay appliqué
and machine
embroidery were all
employed to make this
still life.
(Sandra Francis)

To ensure the success of a piece of appliqué it is important to carry out the necessary preparatory work. The first step is to sketch out a plan of your design. You may choose to transfer the entire design onto a backing fabric, or to cut out the appliqué pieces and assemble it by eye, making adjustments as the work progresses.

Preparing fabrics Whatever your preferred working method, make sure that all the fabrics you intend to use are clean and pressed. You should also check that they are colourfast and pre-shrunk – if in doubt wash a test piece. Finally, check that the grain of the fabric is straight by pulling out a weft thread near one end and cutting along the gap.

Scaling-up your design Once you have sketched out a plan for your design, the next step is to scale it up to the finished size. To do this, either draw a grid onto tracing paper and place this over your design or draw a grid directly onto the design. Then copy the design square by square onto a larger grid or onto dressmaker's grid paper. Alternatively, if you have access to a photocopier with a versatile enlarging facility you could save yourself some time by using it to scale up your design.

Transferring your design If the fabric is fine and light enough, you can transfer your scaled-up design by tracing it directly onto the cloth with tailor's chalk or a fine non-permanent pen. With darker materials you can use dressmaker's carbon paper to transfer the design to the fabric. Note that you must use the dressmaker's type; don't compromise with the office sort – it would mark the fabric permanently.

Another method is to draw the design onto tissue paper and then baste through the tissue paper to the fabric beneath. When the stitching is complete, gently pull the tissue paper away from the fabric, leaving the basting stitches to act as a guide. For fabrics with a pile it is easier to transfer the design to the reverse of the fabric.

Cutting-out the appliqué pieces When cutting, pinning or sewing, work on a flat surface so that the fabric does not pucker or draw. To keep the scaled-up design in one piece, it is a good idea to trace off individual elements onto separate pieces of tracing paper. You can then use these as pattern pieces when cutting the fabric.

Some non-woven materials such as felt, leather and interfacing don't need seam allowances as they don't fray. However, most fabrics will need to be turned under, so be sure to add the appropriate seam allowances to the pattern pieces before cutting out the fabric. Before sewing any pieces into position, turn the edges under, press and baste them.

Storing pattern pieces If you are working on a large project, it is a good idea to store like pieces together in clear, labelled plastic bags to avoid confusion.

Strengthening thread In cases where your appliqué consists of several layers of fabric, or you are using thick fabrics, it is a good idea to strengthen your thread by pulling it along a block of beeswax.

Coping with corners Do not turn under both sides of a corner before sewing. Instead, on an outer corner sew almost up to the angle of the corner, stopping a little before you reach it. Turn under the adjacent side and make a small stitch at a 45-degree angle; then turn in the second side and stitch. On an inner corner, stitch into the corner and then continue on the other side.

Coping with curves and circles When sewing a curve or circle, you will need to coax the material to prevent little corners from forming. One of the best ways of doing this is to make snips all the way around the seam allowance before you begin to sew. The fabric will then give slightly when the allowance is folded under and the piece is sewn into place.

Making crossway strip (bias binding) This haberdashery item is most commonly used for stained glass appliqué. If you make, rather than buy, crossway strip (bias binding) you will be able to use better-quality fabrics and to match – or contrast – the fabric to the rest of your work. Store-purchased crossway strip is available in cotton or polyester satin in a limited range of colours. You can also use home-made crossway strip (bias binding) to pipe or edge items like cushions, pillows or quilts.

To make strips fold a square of fabric into a triangle and mark out parallel lines following the fold at 1 inch (2.5 cm) intervals across the triangle. Then cut out the strips and sew them into lengths. Finally, press under the raw edges.

Making rouleaux strips For a neat finish narrow, long motifs such as flower stems are best made as rouleaux strips. Cut a bias (crossway) strip twice the width you require, adding ¼ inch (6 mm) seam allowance on each side. Fold in half lengthwise, right sides together, and seam. Turn the strip right side out.

Above: This appliqué was made using a combination of stitch and tear techniques (see right) and then embellished with fabric spirals and embroidery stitches.
(Susan Kennewell)

Right: First layer fabrics and machine them into position. Then tear away areas so that their rough, frayed edges become part of the final picture.
(Susan Kennewell)

broderie **p**erse

Sometimes known as Persian embroidery, the technique of broderie perse consists of cutting motifs from printed fabrics, re-arranging them into a new composition and applying them to a plain background. The technique was very popular in England during the 18th century, and in America – especially in the South – in the late 18th and early 19th centuries, as it offered an economical way of reusing expensive imported chintz. By 1800 English and American printers began designing and printing squares of cloth specifically for broderie perse quilts. The most popular of these prints were floral baskets and urns, as well as variations on the tree-of-life motif.

Although there is a general consensus as to the definition of broderie perse, there are many different methods of working. Recent methods include first arranging the pieces, bonding, pinning or basting the motifs in place and then sewing neatly by hand or machine stitching around them. Very fine details are not cut from the chintz, but are embroidered later. Some modern practitioners of broderie perse add wadding to the underside of the motifs to give them some definition.

Left: This broderie perse picture makes clever use of tree branches taken from a printed fabric and arranged so that they frame the house. The size of the flowers compared with the size of the house helps to create depth.
(Rose Verney)

Above: Made in the traditional style, using the broderie perse technique, this quilt is machine appliquéd and pieced, then hand quilted. A crisp fabric like chintz, combined with close-set stitching, enables intricate motifs to be applied.
(Dawn Pavitt)

in*lay* **w**ork

Popular in the 19th century, when it was used to make banners and altar cloths from inlaid brocade and velvet couched in gold cord, inlay work was sometimes known as mosaic work. It has been described as the technique that links true patchwork and appliqué, as well as having similarities to both reverse appliqué and conventional methods. There are several different methods of inlay work.

Whereas applied designs are cut and stitched onto a ground fabric, simple inlay work involves the setting of patterns into a perfectly cut background. The shape which is being inlaid is often cut at the same time as the background fabric to ensure a perfect fit. This technique is often used for wall-hangings or banners.

In the machine inlay, or decoupé, method, two fabrics are stitched together around the outline of a design. The design is then cut away from the top fabric to reveal the motif in the fabric below.

Applied inlay is the addition of narrow panels of contrasting fabric to basic or reverse appliqué, creating the illusion of inlaid work. And reverse inlay is a quick method of producing two similar but contrasting designs by cutting two fabrics together to create two frames and inners; the two pieces are then interchanged, so the one fits into the other.

Above: This wall-hanging features inlaid bird shapes in shot silk, decorated with hand-stitching and gold fabric paint. The entire panel is set into a hand-painted silk border. The bottom edge is finished with hand-made silk thread tassels from which hang painted card shapes.
(Linda Tudor)

Right: This inlay picture, called **Coptic Bird**, *was made in different coloured felts. The four birds were cut out from the four grounds used here and then interchanged with one another. The feathers are worked in chain stitch and the beaks and feet are embroidered using bold red running stitches.*
(Stephanie Gilbert)

Although not traditional, the easiest way to work inlay appliqué is to mount the work onto a background fabric. You can then fit the pieces together like a jigsaw, with positive and negative shapes. Although the best fabric to use for inlay work is a non-fraying cloth such as felt, you can minimize the problem of fraying with other fabrics by applying glue on the wrong side and leaving this to dry. You can also use interfacing; it won't fray, and it can be dyed or painted with fabric paints or pens.

Another method of producing inlay work with fabrics which fray is to turn the cut edges under and finish them with a hemming stitch before applying the motif. This may expose a channel between different fabrics. If it does, you can use a technique that is often employed on Indian appliqué work, which involves sewing a decorative braid, ribbon or cord into the exposed channel to fill the gap.

Inlay work is sometimes described as cut-and-interchange. This is because positive and negative

How to make an inlay design

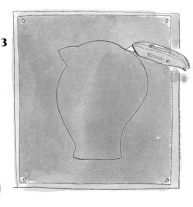

Materials and equipment

- Plain and tracing paper
- Pencil
- Card
- Tailor's chalk
- Sharp craft knife
- Cutting board
- Felts
- Background fabric
- Embroidery thread
- Embroidery needle
- Basting thread
- Beads, sequins or other optional embellishments
- Dressmaker's pins
- Sewing machine with embroidery function (optional)

1 *Draw out your design on paper, marking clearly the area for each individual colour. You should make the shapes bold and easy to cut. Trace over the design using a different piece of tracing paper for each element within the design.*

2 *Using the tracing as a guide, make card templates for each shape in the design and cut them out using a sharp knife. Check the template frequently against the original drawing to make sure that it is still the same size.*

3 *Cut out the foundation fabric and the background piece of felt to the same dimensions. On*

the background piece of felt, position the jug and handle template and then draw around it to produce the design in pen or tailor's chalk. Pin the felt around the edges to a cutting board, then use a sharp craft knife to cut out the design from the felt. Remove the design and retain the background felt.

4 *Baste the background felt, around its outside edges only, to the foundation fabric.*

5 *Draw around the jug template, this time on a contrasting coloured felt. Discard the outer felt and keep the inner piece. Insert the cut-out piece into the felt frame which has been basted onto the*

designs can be produced by alternating light shapes set into dark grounds with the dark shapes cut from those dark grounds set into the grounds that the light shapes were originally cut from. A cut-and-interchange series could consist of just two colours or tones – classic black and white, for example – or it could be a more complex design that involves several contrasting or toning colours.

When working your inlay design you may find that the pieces of fabric stretch, so that the inlaid pieces don't fit the holes exactly. This often happens if you are using felt. One way to overcome this problem is to trace over any gaps and then cut out an extra piece of felt – either in the same or a contrasting colour – to insert. A different solution is to couch the edges of the work, inserting cord, ribbon, tapestry wool or textured yarn to cover any gaps.

If you want to use a thin fabric with a thick one in a cut-and-interchange design, you will have to line the thin fabric with scrim to stiffen it.

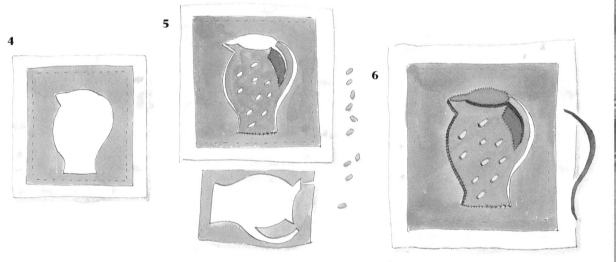

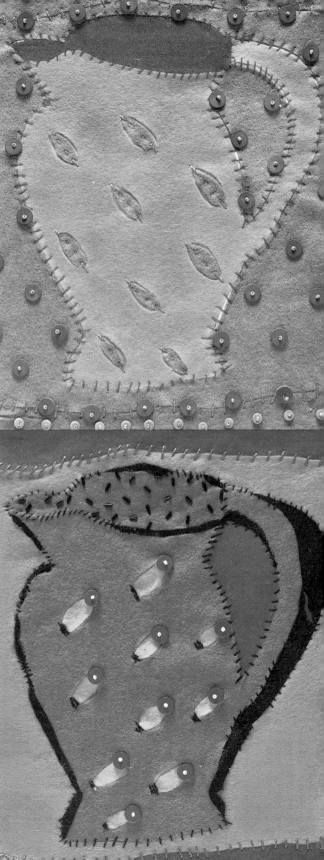

foundation fabric. You may have to ease it gently to fit or even trim it if your cutting isn't accurate. Pin or baste it into position. Now use the other templates and contrasting felts to cut both the handle and infill pieces out in the same way.

6 *Secure all the inner pieces of the jug to the outer felt framework and attach both to the foundation fabric using hand embroidery or hemming stitches. Alternatively, you could sew the pieces together using a machine zigzag stitch. Finally, add decorative details using colourful embroidery threads, beads or sequins.*

Right: These inlay jugs are made from brightly coloured felts. The felt lozenge shapes that are used to decorate the jugs are also cut-out and inlayed. The way that felt stretches has allowed the inclusion of a black shadow in the jug in the lower picture. The decoration of both jugs is a combination of sewn-on beads and simple embroidery stitches. The large wooden beads are held in place with tiny rocaille beads, which are sewn in place with a special beading needle.
(Berjouhie Keleshian)

reverse appliqué

The technique of reverse appliqué, sometimes known as multilayered appliqué, is the opposite of traditional appliqué, in which pieces of fabric are cut out and applied to a background fabric. With the reverse technique, the design is created by cutting shapes out of layers of fabric to reveal the colours beneath. It is thus a process of removing, rather than adding, to create a design.

As an example, in a three-colour reverse appliqué with black, turquoise and orange fabrics, the top layer is orange, the middle one is black and the bottom is turquoise. Start the appliqué by cutting the three layers of fabric to the same size, place them one upon another and then baste them together along the outside edges.

If you want a bit of black in the design, cut out the shape from the orange (top) layer, revealing the black beneath. Where turquoise is needed, cut out the shape from the orange (top) layer and the black (middle) layer to allow the turquoise to show through. As you work, turn under the edges of each cut-out shape and sew them down using a slip stitch and working as close to the edge as possible.

Left: The artist draws motifs onto tissue and lays this on top of a textile sandwich. The outlines are machine-sewn over, then the paper is torn away. Finally, the images are cut from the fabric. (Stephanie Gilbert)

*Above: Influenced by kelims, **Saddle Ochre** is worked in thick fabrics – velvet, needlecord, suedecloth – and so strong zigzag and satin machine stitching is necessary to secure and neaten edges. (Gillian Horn)*

One of the great advantages of the reverse appliqué technique is that colour can be introduced easily wherever it is wanted. By juxtaposing certain colours together, you can create shifting planes and optical illusions similar to those achieved by Bridget Riley in her 1960s geometric paintings.

Although mola work isn't reverse appliqué, but a form of multi-layering combining a variety of cutwork and appliqué techniques, it has a strong use of colour as its essential ingredient. It is therefore a useful reference point when working out how to use colours together in reverse appliqué. Look at examples of mola work to give you inspiration for sizzling colour schemes such as red, orange and black.

Because reverse appliqué is worked in the opposite way to applied appliqué, before you start it is worth planning how the design is going to work using different coloured pieces of paper.

Keep shapes simple, and choose a light, closely woven cloth such as cotton because this will be easier

How to work reverse appliqué

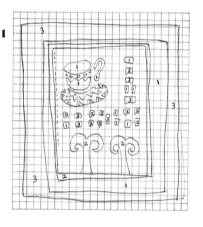

Materials and equipment

◦ *Dressmaker's grid paper*
◦ *Dressmaker's chalk*
◦ *Cotton fabrics*
◦ *Plain paper for template*
◦ *Embroidery thread*
◦ *Sewing thread*
◦ *Basting thread*

◦ *Sharp embroidery scissors*
◦ *Sewing machine with embroidery function*

1 *Sketch out your design on dressmaker's grid paper to make a numbered template. This template for the design shown bottom right indicates (1) the areas you want to be revealed in the plain black fabric, (3) those areas you want to be visible in the black print and (2) those you would like to see in the white fabric. Unnumbered areas will be left uncut in the red fabric.*

2 *Cut four pieces of contrasting fabric — in this case, black print, plain black, plain white and red spot — into identically sized squares. Place the plain black fabric on top of the black print design, then* put the white and then the red spotted pieces on top. Line up all the squares and baste them together around the edges. Using dressmaker's chalk, transfer the details from the template onto the red fabric. Hand stitch around the line indicated in black, using embroidery thread.

3 *Stitching through all four layers, baste around the drawn outline of the black print details.*

4 *Using a sharp pair of embroidery scissors, cut around the inside of the basting stitches through the red, white and black layers of cloth to reveal the black print fabric. Depending on which layer in*

to use than a bulky or loosely woven fabric. You will find that precise geometric shapes are not as easy to make as they are in applied work, especially if you intend to turn the edges under by hand, rather than working with a machine zigzag stitch.

If a small extra area of colour is needed, this could be cut from a separate fabric and machine-sewn into place after all the other layers have been cut away and the edges neatened. When cutting out, use small, sharply pointed scissors and poke them carefully through the top layer of fabric to cut away one layer at a time. If you cut away a layer of fabric you didn't intend to, there are ways of retrieving the situation. Slide in a piece of the fabric that is slightly larger than the opening, then turn under the raw edges of the upper layer over it, sewing them down to secure the new piece. Another way of covering up mistakes is to embellish them with either embroidery or beads. Alternatively, you can add applied pieces over the reverse appliqué work.

4

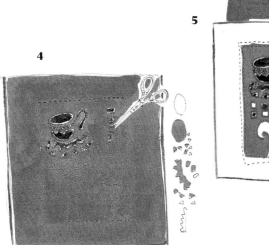

5

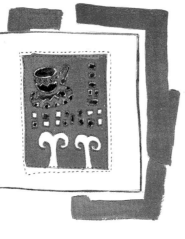

6

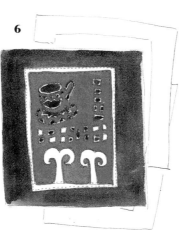

which section of the design you wish to reveal, you will be cutting away either one, two or three layers of cloth. Remove the cut-away layers of fabric. Machine stitch the edges to secure them.
5 *Baste around the outlines of the plain black areas and then with very sharp embroidery scissors cut away the red fabric to reveal the black underneath. Machine stitch just inside the cut edge. Repeat this process with the white areas.*
6 *Once the reverse appliqué process is complete, add detail to the plain white and black areas with machine embroidery stitches.*

Right: Similar subjects, but differently patterned cotton fabrics, were used for these two reverse appliqué pictures. Crisp woven or matted fabrics such as felt or leather are ideal for reverse work. Other fabrics can be used, but those with a marked tendency to fray should be pre-bonded. Machine embroidery can be a very effective way to add an extra decorative element to reverse work. As well, it can serve a practical purpose for finishing raw edges securely. (Stephanie Gilbert)

shadow appliqué

Left: Shadow work is often used with cut work, a technique whereby pieces of fabric are machine-stitched and then shapes cut away from between the lines of stitching. The negative shapes – those that have been cut away – are as much a part of the design as the positive ones.
(Amanda Clayton)

Right: This whimsical shadow appliqué is called **Flying Duckie.** *It is made from transparent fabrics laid over each other so that in some places the image is solid and in others transparent or translucent.*
(Jane Prichett)

In this technique, solid-coloured fabrics are placed on a background. The solid shapes are then covered with sheer fabrics, which may or may not repeat the shape used beneath.

Shadow appliqué may be machine- or hand-stitched; one method uses pin stitch for hand sewing and a close-set zigzag stitch for machine work. Baste a sheer fabric on top of a solid one, matching grains. Then draw the design onto the sheer fabric with tailor's chalk and stitch over the lines. Cut away excess sheer fabric close to the stitching line.

Another method involves cutting motifs from solid fabric, without seam allowances, and gluing them onto the ground fabric. Next, pin the sheer fabric over the entire design and baste around the edges. Then work small running stitches around the edge of each motif. Finally, either sew around the edge of the work so that the shadow work looks quilted, or cut away the sheer fabric at the line of stitching.

Stained-glass **a**ppliqué

Left: This quilt, made by applying commercial crossway strip (bias binding), is based on traditional Celtic patterns. Inspired by a church window, the design has been simplified by eradicating all colour and just uses crossway strip to represent lead. (Rosemary McCloughlin)

Above: Inspired by Celtic imagery, this cushion or pillow cover is an interesting example of stained-glass appliqué. The warm, earthy tones of the patterned fabrics used for the border harmonize well with the fabric used to make the Celtic motif in the middle of the piece. (Jo Ratcliffe)

This type of appliqué has more to do with appearance than technique. Like a stained-glass window, with bright colours surrounded in a sea of black lead, stained-glass appliqué is made of pieces of coloured fabric surrounded by strips of fabric, crossway strips (bias binding) or lines of satin stitch.

There are two main methods: the crossway (bias) or the overlay. With the former, crossway (bias) strips are used to imitate the lead. Because the strips are cut on the cross they have an elasticity that enables them to be manipulated, for example into curves, or to be sewn flat without puckering. It is wise, however, not to attempt to outline shapes that are small or that have sharp corners. The overlay method is in fact a form of reverse appliqué: a dark fabric is placed on top of lighter-coloured fabric and is then cut away to reveal the fabric beneath.

The easiest way to work stained-glass appliqué is to draw the design on the background fabric, then cut out the coloured shapes and pin them to the design. Stick or sew them in place then baste the crossway strip (bias binding) over them and finish using a machine running stitch or hand-worked slip stitch.

How to make a stained-glass design

Cushions or pillows have several advantages as a first appliqué soft furnishing project. In particular, the area to be worked is small and easy to manage, and there is unlimited scope in the choice of fabrics and designs. Also, by tackling a smaller project first, you will quickly learn the important design and the aesthetic considerations that are necessary for taking on bigger appliqué projects.

A stained-glass effect can be achieved by many methods, although the most common technique is to surround brightly coloured fabrics with a much darker edging made of crossway strip (bias binding) or fabric cut on the cross, imitating the lead-work in a stained-glass window.

To create an illusion of stained glass, the choice of colours is all-important. Lorna Moffat, whose work is featured here, uses rich, moody tones. The texture of the fabric is significant: shot or cross-woven silks add a depth of colour that is far richer than a one-colour-weave cloth. The colours change in the light in the way that stained glass does.

Design ideas are sparked off by colours, patterns, or often by just experimenting with a technique, which may lead to unexpected and interesting results.

Materials and equipment

- Various fabrics, such as slub silks and velvets, cottons and chiffon
- Pins
- Tailor's chalk in pencil form
- Thread
- Sewing machine with embroidery function
- Dressmaking and embroidery scissors
- Pillow or cushion pad
- Zipper (optional)
- Paints and dyes (optional)

1 *Choose a mixture of luxurious fabrics in different weights, such as slub silk, rich velvets, cottons and chiffon. Select a variety of colours and patterns, hand-painting or dyeing some if you wish to create interesting effects. Cut all of the pieces of fabric to the same size (the dimensions of the front of the cushion or pillow, including the seam allowance). Create a sandwich of a mixture of fabrics; two or three make a simple, effective design, while more create a detailed, colourful effect. At a later stage* some areas of this sandwich are partially cut away to different depths, revealing a variety of brightly coloured shapes.

Pin the fabrics together and draw the design on the top layer of the fabric sandwich using tailor's chalk in pencil form.

2 *To sew, set the machine to a small running stitch. Using the embroidery or darning foot, drop the feed-dog and lower the foot onto the fabric sandwich. Stitch along all the lines of the design.*

Appliqué is such a flexible medium that new and interesting effects can be achieved just by sewing one shape over another in different ways. For example, a strip of silk can be sewn flat, it can be twisted and caught down, folded, ruched, coiled into a spiral or pleated with other strips. Lorna Moffat appliqués lattice-work strips of silk over a cut-away design to enhance the impression of stained glass in her work.

Appliqué cushions or pillows can be finished off with other decorative elements; consider using embroidery, piping or welting, fringing, braids or tassels to add to the rich effect.

Previous page: The decorative tops of these cushions or pillows were made by machine-stitching together a fabric sandwich of different, richly coloured silks. Areas were then cut away to reveal the jewel-like colours beneath.
(Lorna Moffat)

Right: The fronts for these three cushion or pillow covers were made by using a combination of cut-away technique, as described and illustrated here, and lattice-work appliqué to produce a stained-glass effect.
(Lorna Moffat)

Once the machine stitching is complete, iron the surface flat, setting the iron to the appropriate temperature for your fabric.
3 *Use very sharp embroidery scissors to cut through the layers of fabric as close to the stitch-line as possible, making sure that you don't cut the stitches. You can cut away as many layers as you wish, to reveal as many colours as there are layers.*
4 *To make up the pillow or cushion, use either an envelope design or a zipper closure. To make an envelope type, cut the fabric for the back into two pieces, each the same width as the front and three-quarters its length. Finish the two edges that run across the width of the fabric; these will form the edges of the envelope. With the right side of the cushion-back fabric facing the right side of the appliquéd panel, and the two back pieces overlapping in the middle, sew around the unfinished sides.*
5 *Turn the finished cover right-sides out and fill with a pad.*

m *ixed*
m *edia*

Above: A deceptively simple picture of flowers, made using a variety of small-scale print fabrics. Each flower has been hand-stitched onto the ground and the flower head or leaf has been made using a button.

Right: This piece is constructed from three separate panels of fabric, each with its own forms. It is not colour and pattern, but the use of unusual small beads, ivory fish,

pieces of bone and stars, along with their positioning, which make this composition successful.

Overleaf: The use of old materials, simple images and a few strategically placed buttons makes a very pleasing composition. Note how a house is indicated on the right of the composition by a few simple running stitches on a square of fabric.
(Janet Bolton)

By its very nature appliqué is a combination of media. Even traditional appliqué quilts are a mixture of thread, fabrics, wadding and backing fabrics. Some artists develop the use of mixed media far beyond simply the weights and textures of cloth. The methods of fraying, spray-starching, batik, burning, machine embroidery, dyeing and hand painting are all legitimate appliqué techniques. And you can use materials as diverse as cane, metal, wire, paper, beads, mirrors, sequins, feathers and bone, as well as many different kinds of fabrics, interfacings and webbings. There are no hard and fast rules.

You could combine warm-toned, small-scale print fabrics, like artist Janet Bolton, with a few buttons, sequins, or perhaps a piece of cane to balance a composition. Her work does not rely on embellishments, but the use of, for example, an odd button to make the head of a flower, or a sequin decorating a Christmas tree adds an extra dimension.

Other mixed-media artists combine recycled fabrics with paint and paper and employ paper collage and appliqué techniques to achieve unusual results. One such artist, Jane Prichett, layers transparent and translucent fabrics over solid fabrics. She also mixes her techniques, using, for example, shadow underlay

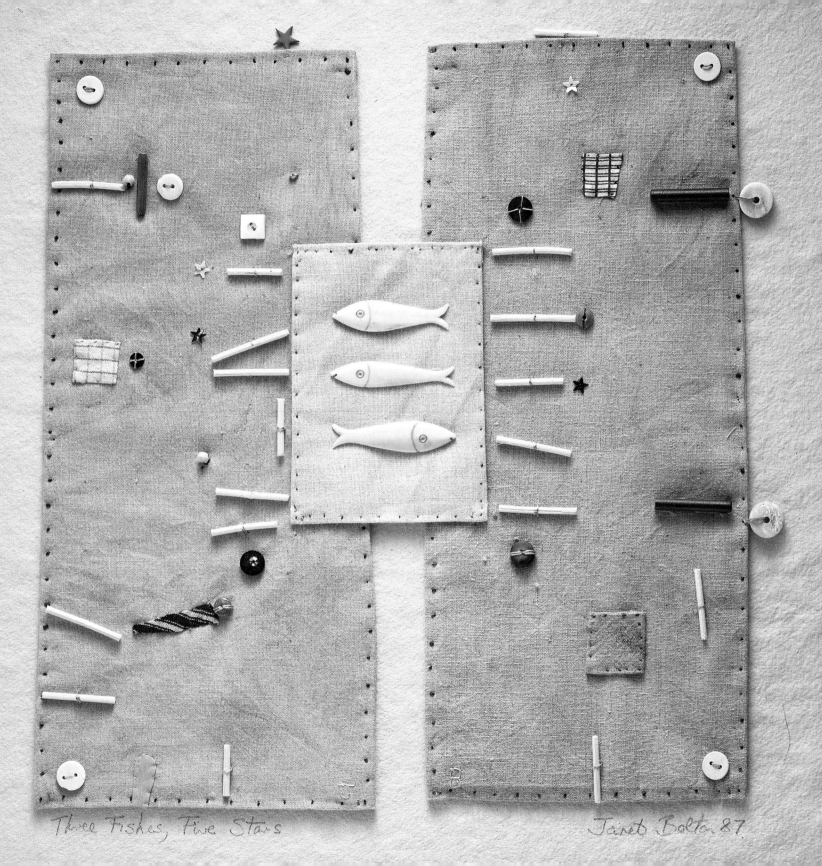

Three Fishes, Five Stars   Janet Bolton 87.

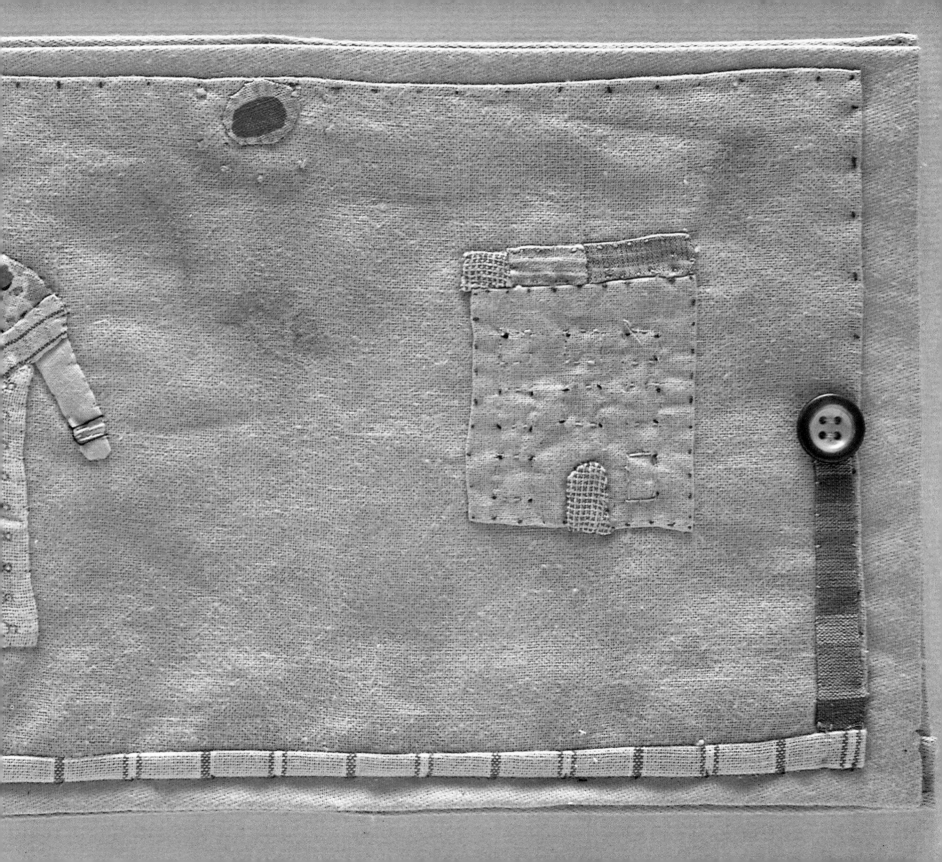

Left: An unusual technique of burning silk in a controlled manner produces shapes which can then be appliquéd onto a background fabric. (Jane McArthur)

Above: The hill is made from a combination of tiny pink squares, hand-sewn on in such a way that they look like woven fabric. The lower part is made from fabric that is dyed to a more intense colour. (Jane Prichett)

and reverse appliqué with a combination of machine- and hand-embroidery. Another artist to combine fabric with paper is Brenda Conner, whose appliqué work is inspired by ethnic fragments, frescoes and antiquities from many different civilizations. Her work consists of distressed paper that is patterned and embellished with organdys (organzas), beads, spangles and hand-stitched metallic threads.

Another popular type of mixed-media appliqué involves using a diverse range of materials with thread and fabric to produce a textile icon that is rich in colour and varied in texture. Artist Karen Howse uses a wide range of media, including cane, wire, metal, paper, beads, thread and fabric, with a variety of techniques, such as hand- and machine-embroidery, layering, wrapping and twisting. Layers of fabrics are sewn and then cut through to reveal the colours and textures beneath. Individual pieces are linked so that edges and spaces become integral to the design.

Fabric paints are an interesting way of adding another decorative element to an appliqué. For example, artist Jane McArthur creates fabric collage from silk that is starched, decorated with spray paint and then burnt into the required shapes. These shapes are then sewn onto a backing cloth and mounted and placed on a hand-made frame.

The variety of fabric paints, inks and dyes available to amateurs and professionals alike is vast. Some will absorb the colour of the background fabric and are therefore only suitable for use on light or white fabrics, while others sit on the surface of the fabric. Some paints, such as glitter types, add textural interest; these are very useful for adding highlights. There are also plasticized paints and others which puff up and stand proud of the surface when ironed on the back. Fabric paint pens come in a variety of thicknesses and can be used to add details where sewing or embroidery may be unsuitable. In addition

Above: This house on a hill is more realistic in form than the one on the left, with chimneys, windows and a roof machine-stitched into place. The background sky is a combination of random running stitches and appliquéd fabrics. (Jane Prichett)

TO18126

to paints designed for fabric, you can use most spirit-based fibre-tipped pens. However, before using them to draw on your work, it is worth testing them on a sample of the fabric to see how it will react. Transfer paints are an easy way of introducing a pattern onto a piece of cloth, allowing you to make mistakes without wasting fabric. You paint the design onto a piece of paper, allow it to dry and then iron it onto the fabric. Simple paint techniques such as sponging, spattering,

come in many shapes, sizes and textures. They may be made from natural materials such as bone, shell or wood. All of these tend to come in natural colours; for more glittery, brightly coloured appliqués, use beads made from glass or metal and sequins. Rocailles, the tiny beads used by North American Indians, are very useful. Use them together to make lines and ridges or dot them about to add texture.

Ribbons are another interesting embellishment

Left: Inspired by decorated medieval surfaces, this work in paper, fabric and thread simulates centuries of decay. The gold threads represent traces of gold leaf on a worn icon.

Right: Silk and tissue paper pieces have been dyed, embossed, cut and printed, then finished with gold. (Hazel Bruce)

and ragging can be used to give depth and texture.

As well as the use of dyed, painted, bleached and otherwise coloured fabrics, the type of cloth or material you use for a painted appliqué is important. Make sure that you match the paint type to the cloth – for example, silk paints will bleed and spread on most fabrics. Check the paint manufacturer's recommendations before you purchase paint and fabric. A few fabrics aren't suitable for painting – felts will usually retain a fuzzy outline when painted or printed.

Another rich source of decoration for mixed-media pieces is a bead or haberdashery store. Beads

you can add to appliqués. They come in many colours, widths, textures and materials. They may be matte or shiny, ribbed or smooth, patterned or plain.

One of the pleasures of mixed-media appliqué is that there are no limits to the experimentation which can take place, and no rules. Mistakes may be over-printed, stencilled or taken out and replaced with other pieces of material, or they may be covered up with a new piece of fabric. You can build up your work slowly by hand, or you may prefer to work quickly using the latest glues, bonding fabrics and machine-sewing and embroidery.

How to make a mixed-media hanging

Textile arts are some of the oldest in the world, so it is not surprising that textiles in the form of hangings, banners and pictures have been used for many centuries to decorate and adorn both domestic dwellings and places of worship. Appliqué lends itself well to creating either pictures which sit in a frame or banners which hang from a rod. Alternatively, as in the case of the work shown here, by Karen Howse, you may wish to produce a piece of appliqué in the form of an "icon," where the box or frame is an integral part of the work as a whole.

Inspired by Indian culture, miniature paintings and scenes of present-day India, Karen Howse's work incorporates the story-telling imagery that is characteristic of Indian paintings. Her work consists of many materials, including wire, cane and thread, which are wrapped, twisted, coiled or bent. She arranges fabrics in layers and then embroiders them by machine. Parts of the fabrics are cut away, and in other places they are slashed with a craft knife to create a worn appearance. Some of the fabrics are customized by tinting them with inks. The artist also

1

2

3

Materials and equipment

○ Sewing machine with embroidery function
○ Cane or dowelling
○ Fabrics – organdy, silk and cotton
○ Inks and dyes
○ Thread
○ Fine (fuse) wire

○ Copper sheeting
○ Tin snips
○ Dressmaking and embroidery scissors
○ Craft knife
○ Ribbon
○ Beads
○ Wooden box
○ Paint and brush
○ Sandpaper
○ Cup hook

1 *Cut pieces of cane to the length required, which will determine the finished size of the work. Paint the cane, then join it to other pieces by wrapping it with wire to create a delicate frame work.*
2 *Use a variety of fabrics including transparent organdy (organza), gauze, silk and cottons. Tint individual fabrics with inks, dyes or pigments to achieve a faded, patchy effect.*

Layer together contrasting fabrics, such as shiny silks and dull gauzes. Stitch through the layers using lines of machine running stitch.

Make separate embroidered pieces in different shapes and sizes: thin border pieces, central square pieces or small repeated diamonds.
3 *Using the sewing machine, create free embroidery without the presser foot. Doodle with the machine to outline figures and fill in vase and urn shapes. Use one thickness of thread but vary the appearance of the line by using straight stitch and zigzag stitch. You can create a thick solid line by using a close-set zigzag stitch.*

By changing threads you can shade and build up

cuts out tiny pieces of metal and traps them in between layers of gauzy fabrics so that they glint when they catch the light.

Although most of the sections within each piece of Karen Howse's work are abstract and based on patterns, the way in which they are assembled forms a composition, often with a pictorial image. Shadow women seem to appear, as do buildings or a squatting figure, all sketched in thread and sitting in their own part of the work. These mixed-media "icons" successfully evoke the traditional story-telling and decorative elements that are present in both Indian and Persian miniature paintings.

By the very nature of some of the elements that they incorporate, mixed-media wall-hangings are often three-dimensional. Today, traditional haberdashery items like ribbons, lace, beads and sequins are supplemented by all manner of materials – anything from artist's papers and paints to metalworker's tin and copper sheeting.

Explore ironmongers, do-it-yourself stores, art stores and other specialist outlets for inspiration.

Right: This intricate picture reflects a love of ancient objects. Various materials – cane, wire, metal, paper, ribbon, beads, fabric and thread – all contribute to constructing this textile "icon".
(Karen Howse)

4

5

6

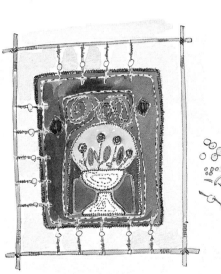

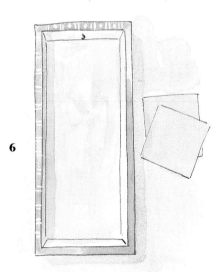

areas of colour. The use of variegated thread gives the effect of a pattern disappearing and mysteriously re-appearing, as the thread changes along its length.

In some of the shapes, trap small spirals of wire and tiny squares of copper plate beneath a layer of organza (organdy), and sew around the edge to contain them in a fabric sandwich. Be careful not to sew over the metal or the needle will break!

4 *Once the fabric pieces have been machine-stitched, some of them can have areas cut away using small, sharp embroidery scissors to create a mosaic effect. Other areas are scored with a craft knife to leave soft, frayed edges like an antique textile. The cut areas are different on each motif to give the design character, just as time wears away and alters the geometry of patterns, whether on textiles or a tiled floor.*

5 *When all the separate elements are made, couch down lengths of cane, wire coils, ribbons or beads on the patches, by hand- or machine-stitching, to form borders, outlines or decoration. Add amulets and charms made from copper plate, wire and thread.*

Right: Portrait panels and architectural detail contribute to the "icon" effect of this textile picture. A custom-made co-ordinating frame or box (6) is an effective way to display three-dimensional appliqué work.
(Karen Howse)

Above and right: These pieces are made from hand-made paper which is distressed and then decorated with pearlized paint. They are hand-embroidered in silks and metallic threads with applied organdy (organza), beads and spangles. (Brenda Conner)

fused **a**ppliqué

Right and above: This natural silk waistcoat is decorated with fused designs of masks and roses. The shadows on the mask's ties are created by lines of machine sewing. The motifs flow into one another, giving a fluidity to the design. The silk motifs are treated with fusible webbing to prevent fraying and to give a crisper finish.
A small rose motif (above) adds interest to the back of the waistcoat. Appliqué is ideal for placing patterns to highlight the cut of a garment. The red rose adds colour to what would otherwise be a rather neutral design.
(Sarah King)

Sometimes known as bonded appliqué, fused appliqué is used as an alternative to sewing for small objects which might be difficult to stitch and for items that are not in constant use, such as evening or wedding accessories. However, this method of bonding fabrics together is more often used as a preparation to sewing rather than as an independent method.

Bonding has been used in the preparation of appliqué for centuries. Of course, the modern equivalents of the early starches and pastes are far easier to use. They come in many different forms, from fusible fabric adhesive to an iron-on interfacing material which is sandwiched between layers of fabric.

Fusible interfacings have a variety of uses. Knitted and loosely woven fabrics such as hessian can be made easier to work by lining them with a fusible material to stiffen the fabric and prevent it from stretching. And by fusing light-coloured interfacing to the back of a light-coloured fabric, you can appliqué it to a dark ground without the ground showing through. As well, interfacing comes in different weights, so you can use it to thicken a thin fabric that is to be applied to a more substantial one.

fused appliqué

How to apply fused motifs

To stiffen fabrics and reduce fraying at the edges of appliqué shapes, you can bond iron-on interfacing material to the back of the fabrics you intend to use for motifs. Because interfacing material is usually white, you can draw the shapes to be appliquéd directly onto it. The shapes are then ready to cut out and sew into position.

Interfacing materials are made in different weights and thicknesses – the heavier the interfacing you choose, the stiffer your motif will be. Special interfacing materials are available for stretch and knit fabrics. Interfacing material is very useful for loosely woven fabrics – they become easier to handle and turned-under edges won't show through.

As an alternative to interfacing material, you can use either spray starch or a fusible fabric adhesive webbing for bonding. Spray starch is best for very flimsy fabrics such as gauze, nets or lawn as, unlike other bonding materials, starch will not show through translucent material. Spray the fabric with starch, cut

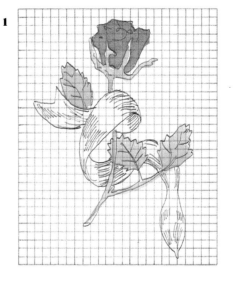

Materials and equipment

- Garment pattern
- Cream silk fabric for garment, as specified in pattern
- Dressmaking scissors
- Fabric for appliqué – red silk
- Gridded paper
- Tracing paper
- Fusible webbing, glue-impregnated on both sides
- Embroidery scissors
- Iron
- Sewing machine with embroidery function
- Thread

1 In general, fashion appliqué is carried out before the garment is made up. Using your chosen garment pattern, cut out the necessary pieces from a suitable fabric – a cream raw silk was used for this waistcoat. Garments like waistcoats and jackets should be lined so that the untidy underside of the appliqué work is covered up. Next, trace the pattern pieces, marking the position of the seam allowances, onto gridded paper. Then sketch out the appliqué design to size, in position on the gridded paper pattern pieces.

2 Trace the design for each motif from the plain paper sketch onto the backing paper of a piece of fusible webbing that has bonding glue on both sides. Group the motifs to make the most economical use of the appliqué material. Following the manufacturer's instructions, iron the unbacked side of the webbing onto the back of the fabric you are using to make the applied design – a red silk in this case. If you can only obtain single-sided fusible interfacing material, you should iron its glued side to your motif fabric at this stage.

3 Using very sharp embroidery scissors, cut out the motif from the sandwich of red silk, webbing (or interfacing material) and its paper backing.

into shapes, then with the starch side facing down, iron the pieces through tissue paper to fuse them to the background. Once fixed, they are ready to be sewn into place.

Fusible fabric adhesive webbing is best for situations where you don't want to use interfacing material, either because you want to keep the result very soft or because you don't want to add to the overall weight of the work by introducing another layer. Most fusible fabric adhesive comes on sheets of thin paper. You place the fabric to be bonded wrong side-up, then position the glued (rough) side of the paper on top of it. To transfer the glue onto the fabric, iron onto the paper, following the manufacturer's instructions for the correct iron setting and timing. Next, peel the paper off. Turn the fabric pieces over so that they are right side up and glue side down and position them on the background fabric. Once you are satisfied with their position, iron each piece onto the background through a damp cloth.

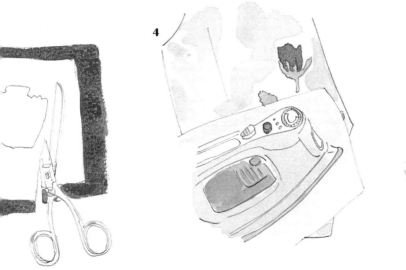

4 *Peel away the paper, then iron the appliqué motif onto the cut cream silk waistcoat pieces. If you are using single-sided fusible material, baste or pin the motif in position.*

5 *Once you have positioned all the motifs, set the sewing machine to the smallest zigzag stitch, and, using a contrasting coloured thread, sew all around each shape to secure it. Change to embroidery thread, set the machine to a small running stitch and "draw" on the fine lines and shaded areas of the design. Once the embroidery is complete, make up the waistcoat, following the pattern instructions.*

Right: This detail shows how the clever use of machine stitching and appliquéd fabric can create a "couture" garment. Professional-looking results are easier to achieve if you use either fusible webbing or interfacing. Note how the artist has used different machine-embroidery border stitches to suit the two motifs. The flowing Art Nouveau-style lines on the mask motif contrast with the uneven, jagged edges to the leaves around the base of the rose. *(Sarah King)*

machine-**S**titched **w**ork

Appliqué that is sewn by machine has different qualities from hand-worked appliqué. It can be quicker to execute, it produces stronger seams and it is more effective if you are using heavier fabrics. Machine-stitching has a "sharper" appearance than the hand-worked appliqué variety, which may have a slightly softer, homespun quality. Machine-stitching is preferable when making articles destined for heavy use, or for items that will be laundered frequently.

Apart from the obvious reasons for using a machine – speed, and for applying one piece of fabric to another – you can also use machine stitching for decoration. Many modern sewing machines are capable of producing embroidery stitches – built-in or freestyle – that will successfully embellish an appliqué. Machine embroidery enables you to produce density of pattern and colour with a speed which would be impossible if the piece were hand-worked.

The most important stitch used in machine-worked appliqué is the zigzag, set close so that stitches form a solid line that resembles satin stitch. This stitch will attach an appliqué motif to its ground fabric securely, with no risk of the appliqué fabric fraying. The width of the stitch may be quite narrow, or as wide as the machine will allow.

Left: Inspired by Parisian gardens, this split image composition works both as individual pictures and as a complete work. Note the extensive use of machine embroidery to create texture. (Maureen Sawyer)

Above: The faces are "drawn" onto fabric with a freestyle stitch; they are then cut out and arranged on the ground fabric and stitched down by hand to create an overall structure. (Caroline Banks)

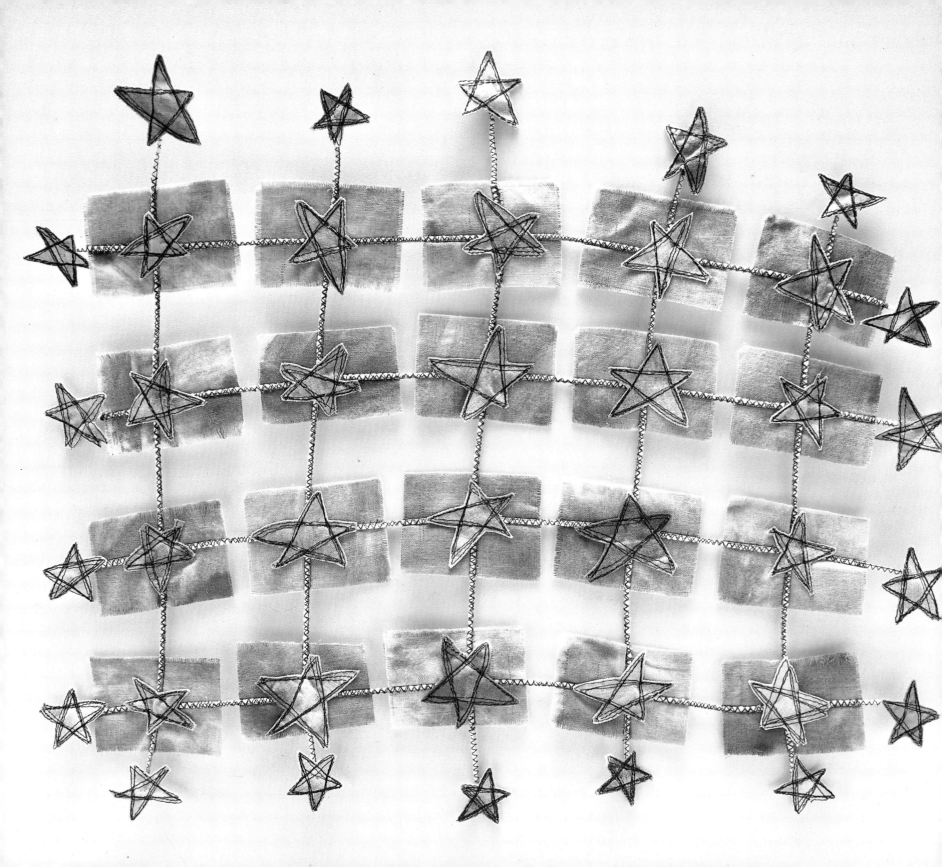

Left: An unusual machine appliqué of stars sewn onto small background squares and held together with a grid of machine-embroidered cord. (Caroline Banks)

Right: The stars, figures and birds in this composition were all machine sewn, then cut out and sewn down onto a background fabric. Worked in white, cream and off-white, they are appliquéd onto a gray background. The machine-stitching is in black to give contrast to the composition and to prevent the images from becoming lost. (Caroline Banks)

Previous page: A selection of the many styles of appliqué work which can be produced with the aid of a sewing machine. A variety of fabrics are included, ranging from fine organdy (organza), glazed cotton, to transparent fabrics. (Sarah King)

Usually, you will either want to match the colour of the thread to one of the fabrics, or you will select a thread that is a shade or two darker. However, if you are applying many different coloured fabrics, you should choose thread that is either the colour of the background fabric or a neutral shade. Satin stitch can be effective for creating a strong contrast to the motif's shape, as in stained-glass appliqué, in which case you should select a thread colour that contrasts with the fabrics you are using.

Satin stitch can look wonderful if it is well done; but if the stitches are uneven, or if there are breaks in the line of stitching, this can ruin an otherwise successful piece. It is important to use a good-quality thread and a sharp needle. It is worth checking your machine's tension by practising on a scrap of the fabric you are working on before you begin. Because a close-set zigzag stitch has a tendency to pull in and distort the fabric, set the tension of the top bobbin slightly looser than the bottom thread, and hold the fabric taut while sewing.

When stitching into corners, you should change to a slightly smaller stitch size as you reach the apex of the corner. Then when you reach the apex, with the needle still in the fabric, lift the pressure foot and turn the fabric to sew the other side. Once you are a few stitches clear of the corner, change back to the width of stitch you were using previously.

Usually, turnings are not necessary when stitching appliqué by machine. The most common procedure is to cut out the shapes to be applied, baste them into position by hand or machine, then sew around the edge of each shape using a running stitch. Next, remove the basting stitches and change the pressure foot to a wide-mouthed one, setting the machine to a close zigzag stitch. Stitch over the line of running stitches, keeping an even pressure and covering both the raw edges of the piece being sewn and the previous line of stitching.

HAND STITCHES

embroidery Stitches

Appliqué designs often incorporate embroidery stitches to give depth and form to a piece of work.

Embroidery can enrich and embellish appliqué; for example, you could use lines of running stitches to build a surface pattern or to enhance, or draw the eye to, a particular motif. Although embroidery is primarily decorative, it can have a practical purpose too; sometimes stitches are used as a means of strengthening flimsy fabrics or to prevent fraying.

Because the appliqué may consist of many thicknesses of fabric, it is important to choose the best thread and needle for the job. The thread should never be so thick as to distort the background fabric, or so fine that it is invisible to the eye. The needle must have an eye large enough to hold the thread, but be small enough to pass easily through the cloth. Also, the fabric to be embroidered must be firm enough to hold the stitches and yet supple enough to allow the needle and thread to pass in and out easily.

Previous page:
This appliqué fabric is made from silk tulle and felted paper, machine-stitched and
cut away in places. The work is finished with feather, chain and other stitches.
(Amanda Clayton)

Above left: Satin, tent and cross stitches decorate this padded silk appliqué.
(Jean Haig)

Right: Herringbone and feather stitches hold together silk, silk tulle and felted linen fabrics.
(Amanda Clayton)

Hand embroidery, whether its purpose is practical or solely decorative, adds a unique touch to appliqués. Certain embroidery stitches are particularly useful for attaching appliqué motifs to ground fabrics; I have described the most popular ones here.

In addition, any embroidery stitches can be used to decorate appliqué work, particularly to add small details or fill in backgrounds. It is worth finding a good instructional book on the subject and experimenting with different stitches. Embroidery will create a very rich effect, but make sure that you don't obscure the appliqué work entirely.

Back stitch

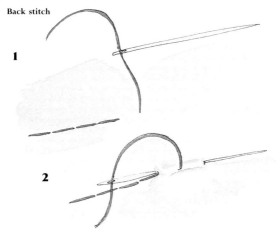

Back stitch

Rather like machine stitching, this hand-worked stitch forms a continuous line of even-length stitches. It is effective for fixing down turned-under and raw edges on non-fraying fabrics such as felt, leather or suede. If you are working with leather or suede, you should use a leather needle and strong thread.

1 Bring the threaded needle through from the back of the work to the front, stitching through all the layers of fabric.

2 Take a small backward stitch through both appliqué and ground fabrics.

3 Bring the needle through again a little in front of the starting point of the first stitch, take another backward stitch and then insert the needle at the starting point.

Running stitch

This frequently worked stitch is used for making lines or outlines. Start with a single knotted thread and draw the needle from the underside of the ground fabric to the front of the appliqué piece, no more than $\frac{1}{8}$ inch (3 mm) from its edge. Make neat, regular-length stitches by weaving the needle in and out through both the appliqué and the background fabrics.

Stem stitch

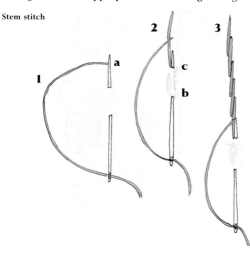

Stem stitch

Worked as a single row, this is a useful stitch for both backgrounds and outlines. It can also be used for filling in backgrounds, when it is worked in parallel multiple rows.

1 Bring the needle through from the back of the fabric to the front at point A.

2 Hold the thread to the right or left of the needle. Then re-insert needle at point B, bring it out at point C, and draw the thread through to complete the second stitch.

3 Keep the thread consistently on one side.

Slip stitch

Useful for finishing turned-under edges discreetly, this stitch consists of a minute straight stitch worked from the ground fabric into the edge of the motif, at right angles to the motif's edge.

Overcast stitch

When making an appliqué, overcasting is one way of attaching motifs to the background fabric. Work this small stitch at an angle to the fabric by passing the needle from the underside of the ground fabric to the front, and then into the edge of the appliqué shape, forming small, diagonal stitches.

Overcast stitch

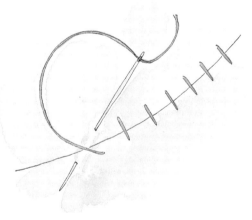

Stab stitch

Sometimes known as pin stitch, this technique consists of minute, even-length stitches that resemble running stitch. But unlike running stitch, the needle is held vertically rather than horizontally – this enables you to pass it through several thick layers of fabric more easily. The disadvantage of this method is that you have to work one stitch at a time.

Attaching sequins

A single bead sewn into the central hole of a sequin will hold it in place. Alternatively, work two or three straight stitches from the central hole to the ground.

Blanket stitch

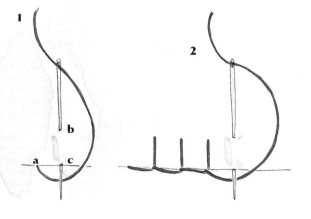

Blanket and buttonhole stitch

Both these stitches are variations on the same technique. When the stitches are worked close together, the effect is known as buttonhole stitch. When the stitches are set further apart, it is known as blanket stitch.

1 Working from left to right, bring the needle through from the back of the fabric at point A. Insert the needle at point B, bring it out at point C, straight down from point B and in line with point A.

2 The working thread is held under the needle as shown, forming a straight line along the bottom.

Left (top to bottom): Running and cross stitches combined with appliqué netting and silks create a lacy effect. Blanket stitch is a decorative and secure method for edging motifs. Running stitch can be used for filling backgrounds as well as attaching motifs.

Right (top to bottom): Edging stitches don't have to be small and neat – large, naively-worked stitches, as if done by a child, can be just as effective, especially if they are worked in vibrant colours that contrast with the pieces they surround.

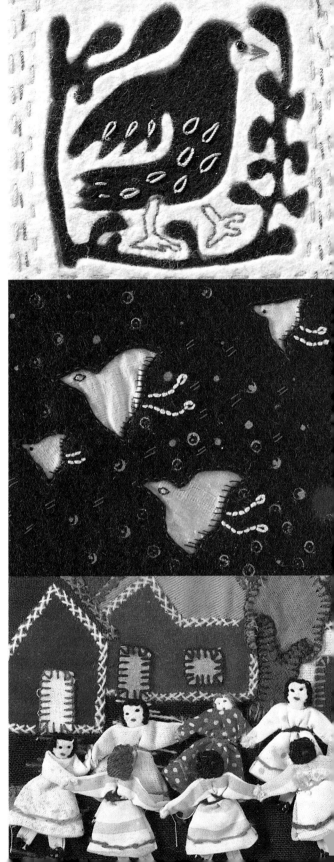

Satin stitch

Although this frequently used embroidery stitch appears to be simple, it is often difficult to get the stitches to lie evenly and close enough together to give a neat edge. Satin stitch is useful for filling, geometric patterns and shaded effects. It can be worked in various lengths, although very long stitches become untidy.

1 To fill in a shape with satin stitch start by drawing a light outline of the shape with tailor's chalk or a pencil. Begin in the middle of the shape, and bring the needle through from the back.

the motif, through all of the layers of fabric. Then work across these running stitches with a band of satin stitches, setting them close together so that they cover the running stitches.

Graded satin stitch

This is another decorative stitch that is useful for finishing the border and covering the raw edge of an appliqué piece. Start by bringing the needle from the back to the front of the ground fabric just in front of the edge of the appliqué motif. Then work satin stitch from the ground fabric into the appliqué cloth in groups of long and short stitches to form a

Satin stitch

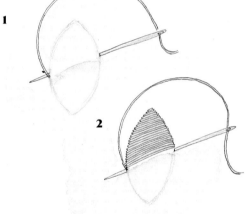

Feather stitch

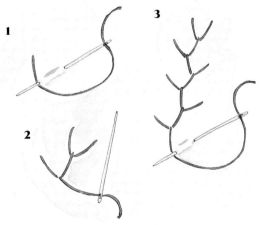

2 To establish an angle (if you want a slant), insert the needle slightly higher on the opposite side of the shape, close to the point where the thread first emerged. Work up to the top of the shape, and then start again at the middle and work down to the bottom. Maintain a crisp edge by working the stitches evenly next to one another.

Padded satin stitch

Underlying running stitches give a slightly raised appearance to this stitch, which is useful for decorating the edges of appliqué pieces. First, work three rows of running stitch just inside the edge of

pattern (for example, three equal-length long stitches followed by three equal-length short stitches).

Feather stitch

Also known as coral stitch, this delicate stitch is feather-like in appearance.

1 Pass the needle from the underside to the front and make a small open-loop stitch to the left, holding the thread down so that it forms a loop.

2 Make the next stitch in the same way, only this time form the loop to the right.

3 Continue working loops alternately to right and left in this manner.

Chain stitch

Use this decorative stitch as a border or outline stitch, or work it in close rows for filling.

1 Start at the top of the line to be stitched and bring the needle through from the back of the fabric at point A. Leaving a loop of thread on the right side, insert the needle again, next to point A.

2 Bring the needle out at point B, just inside the thread loop. The distance between A and B depends on the length of stitch desired. Draw the thread through the fabric, then make the next loop of working thread.

Couching

Two threads are used for this stitch – the first is laid around the edge of the motif while the second is used to stitch it in place. You can use either matching, toning or contrasting threads for this technique. If you use a thick thread or cord for the laid thread it will cover the unfinished edge of the motif in a decorative way. Traditionally, gold or silver cord was used.

Attaching beads

Thread a row of beads, lay them across your fabric and then couch them into position.

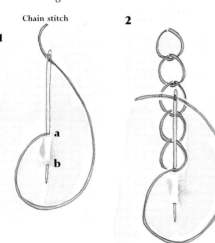

Chain stitch

1

2

a

b

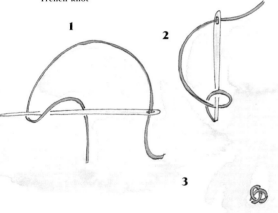

French knot

1

2

3

French knots

Either scatter these knots at random over an area to give a textural effect, or place them close together as filling stitches. The size of the knot depends on the weight of the thread or yarn.

1 Bring the needle through from the back of the fabric. Hold the working thread in the left hand and wrap it around the needle once or twice.

2 Insert the needle right next to the point where you brought the thread through, pulling the twists gently until they are snug but not tight around the needle.

3 Draw the needle through to the back.

Left (top to bottom): Running and satin stitches form geometric shapes on crisp cottons. Feather and buttonhole stitches worked over net and silk appliqué add to the lacy effect created by the fabrics. Chain stitch is very effective to outline motifs.

Right (top to bottom): You can enrich your appliqué work with a wealth of decorative embroidery stitches, as in the top and middle pictures, or just use them in a minimal way to attach motifs, as in the bottom picture, which is still very effective.

SOFT FURNISHINGS

quilts

Left: A modern quilt made in the old commemorative style to mark the wedding of the Prince of Wales to Lady Diana Spencer. (Gillian Clarke)

Above: This quilt was made as a wedding present and includes traditional wedding

motifs as well as subjects with close family associations. (Gillian Clarke)

Previous page: Detail of an intricate appliqué throw worked in both reverse and basic appliqué methods using silk fabrics. (Lorna Moffat)

Over the last 200 years, quilts have been one of the most popular forms of appliqué art. Even with the modern use of duvets, quilting is as popular as ever. Modern materials, especially lightweight, easy-to-wash polycottons and waddings, add to the attraction of quilt-making. New products such as webbing and lightweight interfacings, as well as sewing machines with a wide range of embroidery stitches, mean that quilts can be constructed more quickly than in the past. However, to many quilt-makers part of the attraction lies in the old slow process and they still construct their quilts by hand. Some quilters will work on the entire piece at once; others like to work on one piece at a time.

For the appliqué artist, appliquéd quilts are considered to be the ultimate in quilt design; there is greater freedom than in patchwork as it is easier to produce curved lines in appliqué work, especially if you use crossway strip (bias binding) or cross-cut strips of fabric. There is also greater flexibility in the fabrics that can be used together because, as they are all stitched to the same background, it does not matter if they are of varying weights and thicknesses. The only important consideration when using different fabrics together is whether they are all washable; if they are not the quilt will have to be dry-cleaned.

The revival of interest in quilt-making over the last ten years is a reflection of a general interest in crafts. In the United States, an International Quilt Festival is

held each summer in Houston, Texas, while in England the equivalent is the National Patchwork Championships.

Some of the styles of quilts submitted to these competitions may be seen on the following pages. They are inspired by a diversity of subject matter and worked in a number of techniques, both modern and traditional. Jan Davies's quilt is called "The Big Gamble". It was inspired by part of a poem about someone trying to decide whether to go on holiday abroad or to stay in England. The pinball machine is worked in cotton ticking; the bingo/casino board is stencilled and quilted, and the numbers are embroidered by machine; the score-bells and other parts of the machine have been quilted and then hand-appliquéd. Seaside memorabilia, which make up the lower half of the quilt, combine techniques such as airbrushing, hand- and machine-embroidery and trapunto quilting. The fruit machine is shaped to fit over a pillow, and combines cut-work, appliqué and machine embroidery. The use of red and white striped towelling terry-cloth on the sides gives the quilt a seaside look.

In complete contrast are the quilts of Gillian Clarke, who uses traditional techniques and imagery. "The Royal Wedding" was made on the occasion of the wedding of the Prince and Princess of Wales. It is made in the style of an old commemorative quilt and is worked in a combination of appliqué and pieced work. "Sue and Simon's Quilt" was made for the wedding of Gillian's daughter. It incorporates traditional wedding symbols, hearts, love-birds, love-apples, a wedding bouquet and orange-blossoms.

In the section on stained-glass work there is a quilt designed and made by Rosemary McCloughlin (see page 44). This quilt, inspired by Celtic patterns in a local church window in Dublin, is beautiful in its simplicity. It is worked in squares that each contain a different Celtic pattern. The only colour used is blue,

Previous page: A detail of an abstract throw, the design of which was developed through collage techniques. The strong abstract patterning of this artist's work is based on anti-war themes and feminist philosophy.
(Dinah Prentice)

Right: **The Big Gamble** *was inspired by a poem about vacation or holiday activities. The quilt focuses on the pin-ball machine in the middle. The machine is surrounded by sticks of rock, made from silk, air-brushed with silk paint and then quilted into position.*
(Jan Davies)

Left: A hand-painted and hand-sewn quilt, made from hand-loomed Shantung silk. The work starts with a collage of cut and torn papers. Drawings and paintings are then made from the collage, before the quilt is started.
(Dinah Prentice)

which is sewn onto a natural-coloured background. Gillian Horn also works in reverse appliqué. Her quilt, "Keshan", won her a prize and instant fame in the 1985 English National Patchwork Competition. The design is derived from a picture she has of an old kelim, of which she is a keen collector. The use of rich materials, including velvets and ribbed needlecord, sometimes used the wrong way up, create the feeling of warmth and age, as does her use of colour – a combination of warm browns, terracottas and rust, and the more judicious use of white, cream and black.

The work of Dinah Prentice is unusual for a modern quilt maker as it includes a strong political message. The early American quilts often carried political messages, but they were incorporated in a figurative manner. For example, there are quilts depicting the Boston tea party and ones which carry anti-slavery messages. Dinah Prentice makes appliqué quilts and wallhangings which evolve through experimentation with paint and collage techniques and lead onto finished pieces of work that combine appliqué and pieced patchwork. She started making traditional patchworks at the beginning of the 1970s. Having perfected the techniques, she then began to use them to represent feminist deconstructionist philosophical stances and to show her strongly held anti-war feelings. Although abstract in nature, many of her pieces of work from this time are so strong in their imagery, with long, sharp, phallic shapes in tones of gray and black, that they are quite chilling to look at and immediately convey her anti-war message.

When designing your own quilt, it is worth thinking of the user. Is the quilt for a baby or a child, an adult or a teenager? A baby or child's quilt will be smaller than an adult's, so this is a good project to start out with. Try to incorporate images that have associations for the recipient – for example, a favourite story-time character for a child, a hobby or interest for an adult.

How to make a block quilt

Appliqué quilts are time-consuming to make, and so the design and the preparation is of paramount importance. The easiest way of working is to draw the original design and then to enlarge it to full-scale. Mark the colour of the fabrics on each piece of the design; also number the pieces. Trace off each piece, marking the colour as well as the number on the tracing paper. While working, you can refer back to the original drawing and check the numbers for positioning a particular shape. The tracing paper can be used as a template, or you can trace onto a more durable material such as card if the motif is to be repeated. If you are making a quilt with small, intricate pieces of imagery which you do not feel up to drawing and cutting out, look for the image on a printed piece of fabric, cut it out and use the Broderie Perse method (see page 33) of appliqué.

To work out the amount of fabric you will need place the motifs of each colour together, leaving a ¼ inch (6mm) seam allowance around each motif.

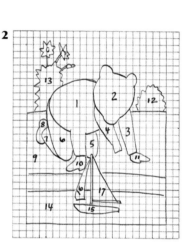

Materials and equipment

- Plain and dressmaker's grid paper
- Coloured pencils
- Tracing paper
- Pins
- Cream-coloured cotton
- Thread
- Needle
- Snaps (press-studs)
- Sewing machine
- Coloured cotton fabrics for appliqué design
- Wadding
- Plain backing fabric

1 Draw and colour the quilt design onto dressmaker's grid paper.

2 Copy the design for each picture onto a large sheet of paper so that it is the size it will be on the finished quilt.

3 Trace off and number each shape. Number the same shape on the large sheet of paper and use this for reference when making up the design.

4 Pin each pattern piece upside-down on the back of the fabric and draw around the shape. Remove the pins and the paper, and then add a ¼ inch (6mm) seam allowance around each shape.

5 Cut out 12 rectangles of plain cream-coloured cotton fabric. Working on one picture at a time, pin the fabric pieces onto each rectangle. Leave a border at the edge of each picture large enough for the frame. Baste the pieces into position and remove the pins. Turn under the seam allowance of each piece as you sew.

6 When all the pieces are sewn into position, remove the basting stitches. Add details, using appropriate materials. For example, a door handle is a snap (press-stud); while the facial features are embroidered. Once all the pictures are complete, cut out the fabric

Measure the entire area for each colour; this will tell you the fabric yardage.

Grace Meijer's quilt for a child, shown here, is called "Rupert in the Attic". This quilt is divided into squares, each reflecting a different aspect of a child's day. If you are making a quilt in blocks, it is probably easier to work one block at a time. Use an embroidery hoop to hold the fabric taut as you sew. When all the sections are finished, sew them together and then add wadding and backing fabric.

Right: This appliqué quilt was designed for a child's bed. The black and green dividing panels represent window panes, through which the onlooker can see the bear engaged in various activities. (Grace Meijer)

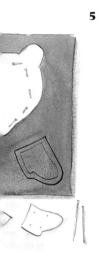

5

6

for the window frame. The green horizontal pieces are cut to the width of the quilt and divided later into sections with the triangular-ended black verticals. Machine-sew the pictures together to form a grid, then sew on the vertical stripes. Cut the horizontal stripes as shown in the photograph and sew these into position. To make a frame, sew triangles of patchwork together to form four strips and then machine stitch this to the outside of the picture grid. Sew plain strips to the outside of each patchwork strip. Baste together backing, wadding and quilt top 1 inch (2.5 cm) from the edge.

Right: To finish the quilt, use a running stitch to quilt around the edges of each square and the outline of each motif. Then add an outside border to the grid of pictures. Finally, sew crossways (bias) strips around the complete quilt to finish the raw edges.

pillows and cushions

Decorative appliquéd fabrics can transform your home; for example, an old sofa can be revitalized instantly by filling it with a clutch of richly appliquéd cushions or pillows or by covering it with a throw-over appliquéd design.

Fabrics soften the appearance of a room; they add both comfort and style. Appliquéd fabrics go further by adding interest and richness of form, texture and colour. Colour can change a room's atmosphere – it can make a dull room seem bright and a chilly one appear warm.

Choose rich, moody tones if you want to conjure up a warm and exotic mood. For this sort of appliqué look for inspiration in art or architecture and use rich velvets and heavy slub silks in greens, deep reds, purples and blues, occasionally shot through with gold. For example, Lorna Moffat, the artist whose work is shown on these pages, is inspired by buildings and spires, vaults, arches and stone columns as well as Moorish and Islamic art. Her work is extremely rich and opulent.

In complete contrast, you could use a selection of plain and/or geometrically patterned primary-coloured or black and white fabrics in order to create a crisp, graphic look, as in the appliqué work of Sarah King (see pages 92-3).

As well, the types of fabrics and motifs you decide to use can add texture to your work. For example, a light and subtle effect can be produced by the clever use of differently textured fabrics in whites, beiges and

creams applied in layers, with some parts cut away and others embellished with embroidery, netting and sheer, lacy fabrics.

It is well worth considering the practical details before you embark on your design. For example, are the materials you plan to use machine washable or will they need to be dry cleaned? Either way, it is best to make your cover with a closure (zipper or envelope type) so that it can be removed easily for cleaning purposes.

Far left: These covers were made by a cut and sew technique; areas were slashed away to reveal contrasting colours beneath. Threads from the base fabrics form part of the design. (Jilli Blackwood)

Left: The design was painted onto wadded silk, then machine embroidered. Next, the silk was applied to canvas and cut velvet shapes were added. (Jean Haig)

Overleaf: A selection of machine-appliquéd cushion or pillow covers. (Sarah King)

GALLERY

a *rt*

Right: A vanishing muslin background for metallic materials creates jewel-like shapes. (Karen Fleming)

Left: A Brittany landscape in which fabrics and colours are built up to capture an impression of light. (Imogen Bittner)

Previous page: Lines of stitching create the illusion of distance on in- and overlaid felt. (Jeanette Appleton)

From the earliest times, appliqué has been used to decorate banners and wall-hangings, in addition to pictures. As well, even when worked for practical purposes – as clothing, bed covers, tent decoration or ecclesiastical robes – appliqué has been a means of self-expression. As much thought has gone into the design and creation of appliquéd artefacts as has gone into conventional works of art.

As with many crafts practised today, the boundaries of art and craft have become blurred. The invention of new materials, the depth of our knowledge of other cultures and the increased ease with which people are able to visit other lands and experience new colours, sounds, smells and tastes all provide inspiration for the creation of original works of art. Not only are we able to see first-hand the treasures of the world – paintings, ceramics, furniture, jewelry – in museums, but much of it is also illustrated in books and magazines.

Most artists' work is not directly representational; their sources of inspiration are merely starting points. It may be the form, the pattern or the colour of an object which inspires you; you may choose only one of these, or all three, to help you create your own

composition. Your work may be an abstract design derived from a texture or pattern such as peeling paint, rusty girders or the wing of a butterfly.

A wider choice of visual references, new materials and techniques and a broader approach to craft, whereby people enthusiastically experiment with many different materials and techniques, have led to a diversity of appliquéd art forms. Much of the work featured in this book could easily fit into the next few pages; on the other hand, some of the artists included here also make so-called "practical" pieces, such as cushions or pillows, accessories and garments.

The sources of inspiration for an artist's appliqué work are as varied as the results that can be achieved. A common practice among artists is to keep a sketchbook in which to note down ideas and to make drawings of things that inspire or trigger-off a new piece of work.

Liz Mundle, who makes pictures and wall-hangings, is strongly influenced by the colours and motifs of the Far East; which in fact is part of her own heritage. Her work is a combination of hand-made felts in rich colours, cut into interesting shapes and embroidered and embellished with shells, mirrors and bead-work.

In complete contrast is the work of Imogen Bittner, who is inspired by the moors, hills and coasts of Cornwall and Brittany, where she now lives. Bittner tries to capture the wildness, light and natural forms of the landscape. Jeanette Appleton, on the other hand, produces abstract and semi-abstract pieces based on the themes of primitive structures, ageing surfaces, patterns of light and the fused images of interior and exterior spaces. Her work combines

felt-making, appliqué, painted silk and recycled papers. The pieces may be framed, but often they are free-hanging, so that they are unrestrained by the perimeter of a frame.

Maureen Sawyer is inspired by many sources: people of different ages, her many trips to Paris, and, more recently, the gardens and houses of the English National Trust. Although Sawyer's work begins from sketches or photographs, the end result is often highly abstract. Much of the work is appliqué- and fabric-based, but Sawyer is no purist – if an image is required, she will achieve it by whatever means necessary, thus her work includes techniques as dissimilar as marquetry and embroidery.

Many of the artists – among them Janet Bolton and Vanessa Blackmore – use recycled materials; this is as much to do with the way that old material has a weathered look or an organic quality as with economy and environmental concerns. Vanessa Blackmore explained: "I use mostly old scraps from clothes. This is a deliberate act as I feel the work takes on an essence of the person who once wore the fabric, the fabric almost takes on a life of its own, attached to it are memories and feelings".

Many different fabrics can be used for appliqué, each producing differing qualities of texture and form. Some fabrics are inherently textural, perhaps with a slub or a loose weave such as linen, or with a pile such as velvet, towelling terry cloth or fake fur. Other fabrics may be chosen for their tactile qualities, from the finest and lightest silks and organdies (organzas) to heavy, smooth slipper-satin, or rough textures like tweed or ribbed needlecord.

Above and right: This ornate series of mixed-media works, entitled **Elizabethan Frame,** *was inspired by the opulent textiles of the Elizabethan period. They incorporate appliqué and quilting, hand- and machine-stitching, with a selection of materials – hand-made papers, calico and interfacing. (Corliss Miller)*

Fabrics may be pleated, quilted, covered in fine stitching or layered; each of these treatments produces a unique effect. Dyeing, burning, slashing, cutting, printing and hand-painting can be combined with more traditional appliqué techniques. Fabrics can be stiffened with spray starch, glue or iron-on webbing; they may be washed and left in the sun to dry, or dipped in a weak solution of bleach or tea. All these processes will change fabric quality and colour.

Left: This picture incorporates embroidery, appliqué and crazy patchwork. The colours are taken from nature and the natural theme is carried through to the "frame" of leaves. (Vanessa Blackmore)

Above: This appliquéd and embroidered panel is made up of tiny fabric pieces appliquéd onto a background fabric, as in crazy patchwork. Fabrics were chosen for their organic qualities. (Vanessa Blackmore)

In all art the importance of both colour and tone cannot be overemphasized. One of the advantages of appliqué is that you can manipulate colour with ease. Another advantage is that, by using transparent and translucent materials layered one upon another, you can create a sense of depth. Complementary colours will add to a harmonious composition, while contrasting, or even clashing, colours can be striking. Much of the appeal in the work of an artist such as Janet Bolton lies in a use of small-scale patterned fabrics. She says that the juxtaposition of fabrics in her work-box often triggers off ideas for her deceptively naive pieces.

Sandi Kiehlman's work is immensely powerful. The image jumps out at the onlooker long before you begin to read the intricate stitching and appliqué which help to form that image. Part of the strength of this particular artist's work is her fearless use of strong, vibrant colour.

Much of Linda Tudor's work has its origins in pattern. Often, she will work a piece on a grid or trellis. This is a method common to textile artists who have trained to design fabrics with intricate repeats and drops. The grid may be made up of pieces of hand-dyed card or fabric, richly embellished with gold and copper powders and silk embroidery threads.

The variety of techniques and results that the artists featured in this book have produced should encourage anyone setting out to create their own work. It is by just such experimentation with materials, techniques and images that you will create your own art.

 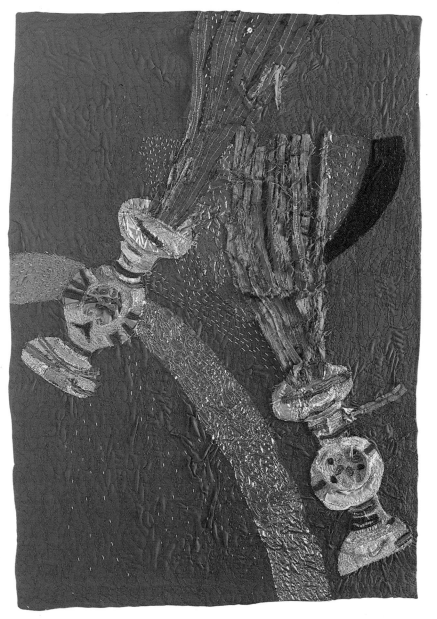

Above and above right: The menacing-looking gentleman and the burning candles in *their sticks are built up with appliqué and embroidery. (Sandi Kiehlman)* *Right: A mixed-media appliqué using diverse materials – wood, card, fabric – and techniques* *– gluing, machine-and hand-stitching and quilting. (Maureen Sawyer)*

wall-**h**angings

From earliest times, dwellings have been decorated with wall-hangings which have included appliqué work. When creating a hanging, the style of the finish is almost as important as the design of the hanging itself. When you plan your design you should take into account how you will finish the edges. You can choose between binding them with either crossway strip (bias binding), purchased braid or ribbon or else turning them under.

Also, you must consider how the hanging is to be suspended. You can sew a channel to the backing fabric to take a rod hidden behind the work, or you can make loops from the border of the hanging to hold a piece of dowelling or a decorative rod above the work. You may wish to add further interest to the hanging by trimming it with a decorative edging such as bought or hand-made braiding, fringing, ribbons, cords or tassels.

Previous page: Inspired by kelims, Saddle Ochre works as a wall-hanging, quilt or throw. (Gillian Horn)

Above: Markings are arranged to radiate from the central zebra head. (Veronica Double)

Right: A felt hanging inspired by travels in India. The artist uses bonding techniques, basic and inlay appliqué, hand- and machine-embroidery, beads, metal trimmings and tassels. (Liz Mundle)

FASHION

c *lothing*

Appliqué has been used to decorate clothing in many different countries throughout history. For example, in the late 1960s there was a vogue in Western countries for "ethnic" clothing from the Indian subcontinent, which was decorated by hand with appliquéd motifs and mirror-work.

Folk art is fashionable once again, so it is worth looking at folk designs for inspiration. For example, South American mola work (see p.113), a complex multilayered combination of cut and applied work, can be used to produce richly decorative garments. Mola is the Kuna Indian word for "cloth", but it is often used to mean the front or back panel of a blouse as well. Mola work is often mistakenly referred to as reverse appliqué. But molas are built from the base up; each layer is finished before the next is applied. In each layer, more shapes may be applied or cut away. Traditional designs are strong and colourful, with imagery based on mythology.

However, it is in the high-fashion houses of Paris, Milan, London and New York – where the cost of creating a garment is unimportant, and a designer can indulge him- or herself at the customer's expense – that the use of appliqué has been, and still is, strongest. Happily, the cost is in great part related to the skill and time involved in the work, therefore if you can acquire remnants or scraps of expensive fabrics for little or no cost you can create a couture appliqué garment at home.

The undisputed home of couture appliqué is in Paris. The main reason for this is the proliferation of

Previous page: An appliquéd dress fabric made from netting, ribbon, beads, glass and diamanté. The pieces are assembled by gluing and sewing.

Right: This dress is made from appliquéd lace and netting, dyed and painted gray and silver and decorated with ribbon roses, stones, sequins and beads.

Left: The canvas bustier base for this dress is appliquéd with paper lace and netting. The front panel features mirror glass and sequins. The skirt was made from clear plastic and netting. Once constructed, the dress was sprayed with gold and glitter. (Kerry Avis)

specialist craft workshops, where, since the 1850s, high-quality trimmings, embroideries, appliqués and artificial flowers have been made for the haute couture houses.

It is worth studying the work of these crafts people, both as a source of design ideas and a guide to technique. Look at the work of one of the great couturiers of the early 20th century, Paul Poirot, who commissioned many young artists, such as Raoul Dufy and Jean Dorville, to design stunning appliqués and embroideries.

It was from La Maison Lallement, the craft workshop set up by Felix Lallement, that the best appliqué and embroideries originated. From 1898 to 1950 he supplied the top designers with work created from a number of techniques and materials, including appliqué in fabric and leather, drawn-thread and raised cord work. The workshop created two collections a year of about 200 designs. Samples were made on fabric panels that imitated the flat front of a dress. Only the finest fabrics — silks, velvets, brocades, georgette and chiffon — were used. They were put together in startling combinations to emphasize texture. Fragile silks were combined with deep-pile silk velvet and gold and silver lamés were overlaid with cobweb-thin metallic lace.

Rich patterning — geometrics, florals — has been a part of fashion appliqué for centuries. A newer theme, which first emerged in the second half of the 1930s, is the extravagantly escapist use of appliqué that takes its inspiration from modern art. The person largely responsible for leading fashion into a world of fantasy was Elsa Schiaparelli, whose work was often ornamented with surrealist images appliquéd onto garments. With the artist Salvador Dali, she devised a dress patterned with *trompe-l'oeil* tears, a hat like a shoe and a chest-of-drawers dress. As well as art, other media have had an influence on fashion appliqué. Hollywood in the 1920s and 1930s, with its

Left: These custom-made silk items are decorated with fused appliqué patterns and finished with machine embroidery.
(Sarah King)

Above: This waistcoat is made using a modern version of the traditional mola work produced by the Kuna of South America.
(Herta Puls)

extravagant musicals and ornate costumes, was an ideal place for costume designers with a penchant for the highly decorative.

Appliqué resumed an important place in the history of fashion in the 1970s in the work of British designers like Bill Gibb and Zandra Rhodes. Gibb's work was very feminine and included the use of fine fabrics. Rhodes also uses delicate fabrics – soft silks, fine satins and tiny beads – as embellishments. During the 1970s and 1980s, many other international designers included appliqué in their work. For example, the Italian designer Krizia featured appliquéd wild animals draping the shoulders of his models. He created some of the most popular and most copied appliqué designs of the 1980s. In France, Christian Lacroix and John Paul Gaultier have both used appliqué on all manner of garments. While in England designers like Workers for Freedom have drawn inspiration from traditional folk appliqué to produce high fashion dirndl skirts and waistcoats.

Appliqué continues to be an important and exciting element of fashion; the results are very often not only beautiful works of art, but also designs with a timeless quality. Appliqué is a particularly suitable technique to use when making special occasion garments such as wedding dresses, ball gowns and evening jackets or wraps.

accessories

As with clothing, appliqué is a popular technique for decorating accessories such as shoes, hats, belts, fans, handbags, purses and jewelry. One of the advantages of using appliqué for accessories is that the weight of the object may be as light or as heavy as required, depending on the fabrics used. For example, long, dangling earrings comprised of a web of fine fabrics and inset with small beads will not be uncomfortable to wear. As well, you can make items like belts, bags or hats from fabrics that match, or contrast with, existing outfits. And appliqué is ideal for creating accessories to match special occasion garments such as wedding dresses or ball gowns.

Shoes

It was not until the late 1970s that appliqué played an important part in shoe design. The shoe fantasies of Thea Cadabra are some of the best examples of the imaginative use of appliqué on shoes. In the mid-1980s, the Italians revived leather appliqué on shoes, often further embellished with diamanté, studs and ribbons. Try using appliqué to decorate ready-bought fabric-covered shoes – wired motifs or bonded appliqué designs using non-fraying fabrics, beads, ribbons or sequins are all appropriate. And home-made soft fabric shoes – for example, slippers or babies' bootees – can be decorated with appliqué.

Hats

Millinery has always had applied trimmings; whether this is true appliqué is debatable. However, artists such as Sandra Grant, Sarah King and Jilli Blackwood make truly appliquéd hats. Sandra Grant's hats are made of wired and textured appliqué surfaces, which are twisted to support petals, stamens and leaves. The fabrics are fine and laid over one another, creating a soft, semi-transparent finish. Sarah King's designs involve the use of a combination of machine embroidery and fused appliqué. Jilli Blackwood makes hats in the same way that she designs her cushions, pillows and wall-hangings. Her technique involves using layers of richly coloured fabrics, some of which are cut away to expose the fabrics beneath.

Jewelry

Soft appliqué jewelry has the advantage of being light to wear and inexpensive to construct. A wide range of results can be created – from filigree brooches to geometric-patterned earrings. You can match fabrics to garments or create any number of effects by experimenting with new materials such as dissolvable muslins.

Overleaf: These original hats are made from custom fabrics which were hand-dyed, layered, cut and slashed, then decorated with machine embroidery. Wire is used between the layers to give them shape. (Jilli Blackwood)

Right: These pill-box hats are all decorated with fused appliqué motifs and machine embroidery. The edges of each hat reflect the designs on the crowns. A line of piping gives a neat finish to the join between the crown and brim. (Sarah King)

How to make a hat

Wired appliqué is a term used to describe the process of attaching wire to fabric so that it can be manipulated to create numerous freestanding shapes such as flower petals or shells. Natural forms, including plants, landscapes and the sky, are frequently used as inspiration for shapes. This form of appliqué is an exciting departure from conventional flat textiles.

It is possible to use almost any fabric for wired appliqué as long as the sewing machine can stitch through it. You should employ finer fabrics for more delicate subjects such as flowers. Select at least three different colours, making sure that one is a shade of green or blue-green for the stems and stalks. If you can't find the right shade in a pre-coloured fabric you can achieve the effect you want by dyeing the cloth at home. Apply the inks or dyes either before or after each form is constructed.

Muslin is a particularly suitable fabric for wired appliqué. Not only is it semi-transparent but it holds colour nicely, giving a soft appearance even to the brightest hues. For a more consistent texture, use a sturdier fabric or line the muslin with interfacing.

Equipment and materials

∘ Wire of varying thicknesses (cotton-covered wire can be coloured to blend with the fabric chosen).
∘ Embroidery hoop
∘ Fabric inks, paints or dyes
∘ Pins
∘ Scissors
∘ White (PVA) glue
∘ Paint
∘ Sewing machine with embroidery function
∘ Needles
∘ Green and coloured threads
∘ Fabrics – muslin and iron-on interfacing

1 To make the petals bend a length of wire into an oval shape and attach it to the fabric using a sewing machine set on a fairly long zigzag stitch. Guide the wire under the foot of the machine, stitching over the top of the wire to secure its position. Trim the fabric back and stitch again with a satin stitch to hide loose threads and fraying, as you would do in ordinary appliqué. Make about five petals per flower.
2 Carefully study the stigmas and stamens of the flower and imitate them using wire and inks. Fold over the tip of a small stem of wire and fill in this end with a little white (PVA) glue and paint of an appropriate colour. Leave to dry. Make the stigma in a similar way, or attach a very small piece of fabric to the end and secure with white (PVA) glue mixed with paint of the appropriate colour.
3 Use thicker wire to make the stalks. Cut strips about ½ inch (1.25 cm) wide from your chosen fabric and wrap the strips around the wire. Neaten with some white (PVA) glue mixed with water. Join all the stigmas and stamens together by wrapping them to the stalks with green thread. To join the

As the fabric is sandwiched together with the wire, you can use a mixture of materials with contrasting textures. For example, a satin overlaid with a muslin will give a faint sheen, while slub silk, with its ridges, will mimic natural textures such as bark.

Bear in mind that the finer the wire you use the more malleable it will be and the easier to machine stitch into place without breaking needles. However, fine wire will not hold its shape as well as wire of a thicker gauge, so you will need to hand-sew thicker wire to the edges to form the finished shapes.

Top right: This cloche hat is reminiscent of the designs that were worn in the 1930s. The crown is made up of layered fabrics. The dyed muslin which forms the rolled-up brim is stitched, cut into strips and woven into a twill design.

Bottom right: Pinky mauve flowers set on a bed of peacock, hyacinth and cornflower blue create this lively effect. This design has a light feel for in many areas there is only one layer of transparent fabric. (Sandra Francis)

4

5

petals to the stalks, hold them in place and secure with a few stitches. Then wrap thread on top until the join is completely disguised. Make the leaves in the same manner as the petals, but create a longer, thinner shape.
4 *To create the background for your wired flower sculpture, machine embroider freestyle onto a patchwork of different fabrics, blending across all the joins. The needle of the sewing machine acts as a paintbrush and the coloured threads selected form the palette of colour. To make the transparent trim*

stretch transparent fabric onto an embroidery hoop and embroider the pattern directly onto the fabric. Then stitch wire onto the back of the fabric and disguise with inks of the appropriate colour.
To make up your appliqué work into the background for the hat, join the patchwork and transparent fabrics together and stitch strong wire to the back. Then shape the wired fabric onto a milliner's bowl.
5 *Attach the flowers to the hat by bending them into the desired position. To secure them, stitch down the main stems firmly by hand.*

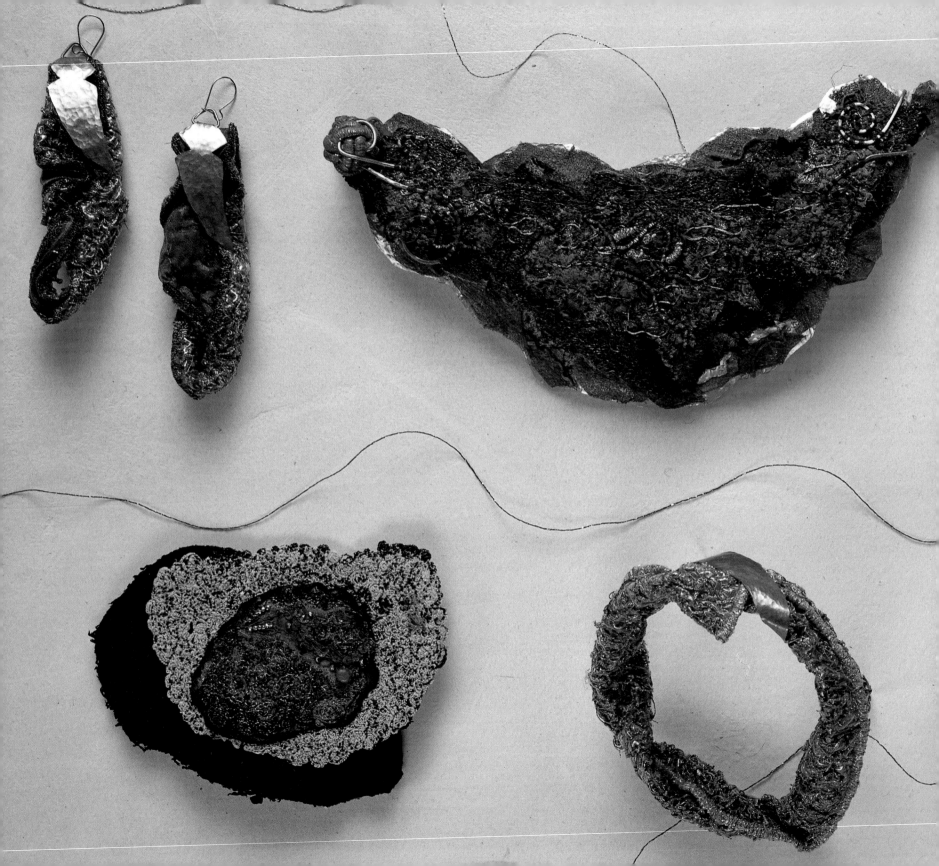

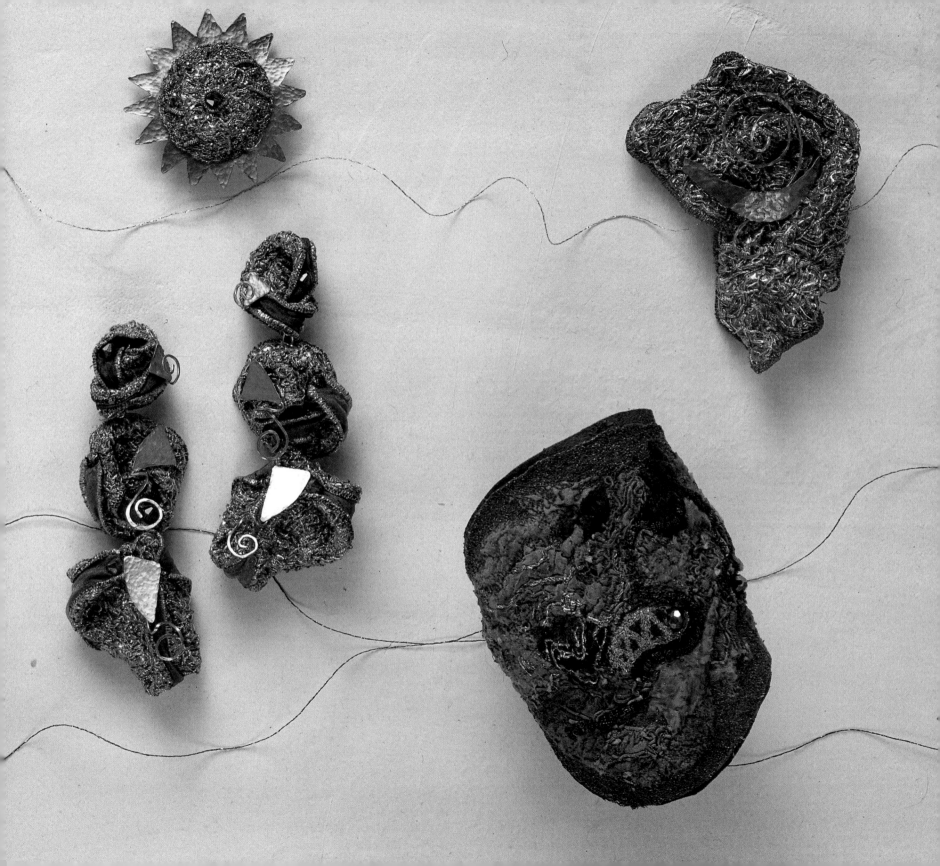

How to make appliqué earrings

Appliqué is an interesting technique for making jewelry. Unlike jewelry made with other media, the results can be very light. You can use wire as part of its construction to produce a malleable, mouldable surface. Another method consists of fusing a layer of fabric, or other materials such as feathers or sequins, onto a backing of fusible webbing. This latter technique is used in making sequinned tiaras and feathered masks for festival or theatrical wear.

A third technique, illustrated here, involves the construction of a special material by sandwiching layers of different fabrics between plastic and water-soluble fabrics and fusing them together in hot water.

Because the technique of appliqué is so flexible, jewelry can be made to imitate other materials. For example, by using iridescent and metallic-coloured lamés and tissue lamés, set with paste stones such as fake rubies, emeralds, sapphires and diamonds, you can achieve extravagant and spectacular results.

You can make many different kinds of jewelry using appliqué techniques – from chokers and neckpieces embellished with beads, spangles, netting

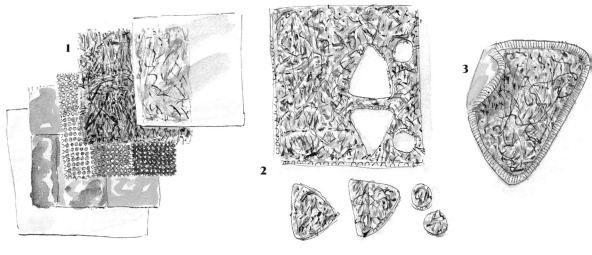

Materials and equipment

- Hot-water soluble fabric
- Silk fabrics in various colours
- Sequin waste
- Gold thread or wire
- Embroidery and sewing threads
- Clear plastic (PVC) sheet
- Thin copper sheet
- Tin snips
- Beads
- Fine (fuse) wire
- Scissors
- Sewing machine with embroidery function
- Jewelry findings

1 *To prepare the base material, cover the bottom layer of hot-water-soluble fabric with squares of two-tone silk in different colours. Next, add a layer of cut squares of sequin waste in different colours, followed by a layer of cut-up threads. Use lustrous coloured threads, metallic threads and colourful embroidery threads. Place a layer of transparent plastic (PVC) fabric over this.*

Next, use a sewing machine with an embroidery function to stitch the sandwich layers together with gold thread. Wind a thick gold thread on the bobbin

spool and thread the machine with a multicoloured cotton. Turn the fabric sandwich upside-down, so that the water-soluble fabric is on top and stitch a close random pattern all over, using a freehand embroidery stitch. (The gold thread will appear on the top layer of fabric.)

2 *Cut out the fabric sandwich into shapes for the jewelry – 2 triangles and 2 circles for these earrings. For each shape, cut a piece of hand-painted or dyed silk to the same size.*

3 *Thread the sewing machine with one coloured*

and flowers to bracelets, brooches and earrings. As a technique, appliqué is particularly useful for making jewelry for stage productions because you can use it to simulate expensive materials.

Appliqué jewelry may also be purely abstract and sculptural. The pieces featured here were inspired by artefacts which have changed with age, in particular ancient ceramics, and the way in which they are affected by time and weathering. The finished appliqués are turned into jewelry by attaching findings to the back of each piece.

Right: This jewelry was made from silks combined with machine stitching and sandwiched between dissolvable fabric and plastic. Each piece is then moulded into shape and embellished with gold stitching. (Judy Clayton)

Previous page: This collection of appliquéd jewelry is based on a specially constructed fabric, described here, which is then embellished with other materials such as cut metallic shapes, embroidery and beads. (Judy Clayton)

4

5

thread on the top and another on the spool and then satin-stitch the silk to the back of the fabric sandwich. (Loosen the lower tension so that both coloured threads are visible on the top of the work.)
4 *Submerge each shape in boiling water. The hot-water-soluble fabric inside will react by shrinking, pulling together the sandwich of textile material and plastic. The surface will become bumpy, ruched and textured. Leave the shape to cool slightly, then mould it by hand while still wet and pliable. Flatten, or pin down the corners or make folds.*

5 *To make the shapes into earrings, add hand-sewn beading and stitch rows of running stitch in metallic thread, then stitch goldwork wire or thread in a pattern over the surface. Sew the finished circles onto purchased jewelry backs.*

To make the hanging part of the earring, glue beads, wire and brass or copper shapes (cut these from metal sheeting using tin snips) to the triangular pieces. Sew on a hand-made hook to link the lower, triangular part of the earring to the circular piece.

Handbags and purses

In the 19th and early 20th centuries bags were made from fabric decorated with beadwork, embroidery and appliqué. They were also made from fine leather, hand-dyed in vibrant colours and decorated with leather appliqué work or interwoven leather strips. Shoes and gloves were decorated in a similar manner, often to match a particular dress or outfit.

Many contemporary makers of appliquéd handbags have a different design approach: the accessory is considered of value for itself rather than as an appendage to a dress or suit. Linda Tudor, who makes both appliquéd pictures and handbags, creates her bags with as much care as her pictures, using similar materials and techniques so that the bag or purse is a work of art, just like the picture.

Fans

Fashionable throughout the 18th century, the popularity of fans began to fade in the early 19th century, when the designs tended to be plainer. However, there was a revival at the end of the 19th century, during the 1880s, when large and highly decorated fans, with full-blown applied roses and steel spangles, were produced.

Juliet Helen Walker is a present-day maker of fans. Like many of those made in the 18th century, the body of her fans are constructed from paper. The fans' edges are treated with a combination of materials, using both traditional and new techniques. The embroidery is worked onto a water-soluble fabric, which then dissolves in boiling water. The embroidery, which is a combination of surface stitching and appliquéd transparent fabrics, is then applied to the fan and further decoration is added in the form of bead-work.

Appliquéd fans can be used to accessorize a formal party dress, but most people display these delicate and beautiful works of art on the wall, as they would a picture.

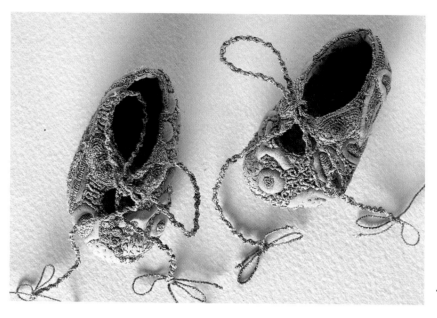

Top left: The cotton for these booties was hand-dyed to create a multicoloured effect. They are padded and embellished with cord appliqué and gold threads. Inside the booties, tiny multicoloured stitches are worked in cotton embroidery thread. (Claire Johnson)

Bottom left: This black felt purse is decorated with bonded silk shapes and Indian silk crossway (bias) strip. (Linda Tudor)

Right: A pair of hand-held fans made from treated paper with applied embroidered and beaded edgings. (Juliet Walker)

THREE-DIMENSIONAL APPLIQUÉ

S*tructures*

The term three-dimensional appliqué is used to describe a wide range of work. It may be employed to refer to clothing, accessories and wall-hangings, as well as to sculptural forms. Indeed, true appliqué, whereby one fabric is sewn onto another and thus stands proud of the background, is genuinely three-dimensional. When used for clothing textiles, it is a refreshing change from conventional flat fabrics.

Historically, Elizabethan stumpwork was a form of three-dimensional appliqué in which ornament was raised in relief on a foundation of wool or cotton fibre. A fine 17th century example, called "David and Bathsheba," can be seen in The Victoria and Albert Museum, London, England. Three-dimensional appliqué is used as decoration on many ethnic artefacts that are exported to Western countries. For example, it appears on slippers from China and Africa and wall-hangings and sweaters from Chile.

Many contemporary appliqué artists experiment with the three-dimensional aspects of appliqué. For example, the work of the artist Dot Linton, partly inspired by old-fashioned dressers, stoves and kitchens, is constructed mainly from handmade felts onto which she machine stitches, embroiders or applies strongly contrasting fabrics such as satin. Sometimes her work is in the form of wall-hangings, at other times it is freestanding. There is often a surprise element, for example a mouse or frog hidden behind a door. It is the three-dimensional quality combined with contrasting textures, rather than the colour, which gives her work its charm.

Previous page: The base fabric is several layers of muslin, dyed and machine-stitched to add texture. The tulips are made in the same way, using inlaid wire to form shapes. (Sandra Grant)

Above: A felt appliqué inspired by kitchenware

– the design portrays a dresser. (Dot Linton)

Left: The side panels of these soft pots are individually made and embroidered. They are stitched together and then sewn onto a weighted base. (Stephanie Gilbert)

How to make a 3D picture

Materials and equipment

○ **Linen or burlap (hessian) background fabric**
○ **Fabrics for appliqué – rust, yellow and green satin, black corduroy, printed patchwork quilting, black organdy (organza), white cotton calico, gold tissue lamé**
○ **Grosgrain (petersham) ribbon**

○ **Polyester batting (wadding)**
○ **Sewing machine**
○ **Scissors**
○ **Thread**
○ **Wool**
○ **Metallic thread**
○ **Gold cord**
○ **Fabric paints**
○ **Crossway strip (bias binding)**

Although not completely three-dimensional, the piece featured below does contain a three-dimensional element. It is similar to a wall plaque, being a flat-backed object designed to hang on a wall, with all the "action" taking place on the front. The success of a piece such as "What Happens Now, Goldilocks?" is that it can be read from a distance as well as being interesting under closer scrutiny.

In work such as this there is plenty of opportunity to explore different dimensions and shapes. For example, doors can be made to open and close, hiding or revealing appliquéd contents. The use of free-floating appliqué in a three-dimensional piece is worth considering. In this work the top of the picture is covered with a network of fabric branches and leaves, all of which are caught only by the stems, so that

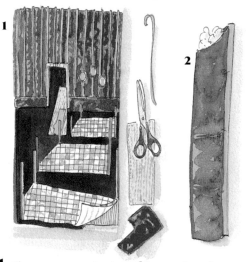

1 *Choose a strong backing fabric such as linen or hessian which will take a great deal of weight. Sew the flat details onto what will be the background. In this case a rust-coloured satin was used for the walls, with green grosgrain ribbon (petersham) forming the stripes and a black corduroy for the floor. The bedcovers are made from a printed patchwork fabric pre-quilted with wadding and then sewn into position (leaving the bottom of the bed in which Goldilocks will sleep open). Next, sew the doorway; make the panel of light in the doorway from a translucent fabric. Now sew on the bed legs, which are made from grosgrain (petersham) ribbon. Make the portraits by cutting small ovals of cotton cloth, painting on the faces with fabric and then outlining in gold running stitch. Sew each portrait*

onto the "wall" and slipstitch gold cord in place to make their frames.
2 *Make the padded door frame from the same fabric as the background wall. Place the fabrics right sides together, sandwiching between them the green grosgrain (petersham) ribbon that forms the outer edge of the doorway. Machine-stitch through fabric down the inner edge. Next, put the stuffing into position. Hand sew the bottom of the frame closed.*
3 *Cut the bear's body from gold tissue lamé, with his righthand arm as a separate piece. Machine-sew him into the doorway using a running stitch. Hand sew his separate arm over the padded door frame.*
4 *Make the frame for the edge of the hanging using the same method as the doorway. Slipstitch the gold cord in place. To make the leaves use various fabrics*

they curl just as real leaves do with age or movement by the wind.

Layering of elements in a design is another approach that will enhance the three-dimensional quality of your work. Here, the padded frame has the appearance of a conventional picture frame, yet an element of the picture – Goldilocks's hair – cascades out of it and over one corner.

Right: Synthetic polyester batting or wadding is a versatile, washable material that is very effective for creating a three-dimensional appliqué.

Right: This three-dimensional wall-hanging is called **What happens now Goldilocks?,** *and is based on the old-fashioned fairy story of* **Goldilocks and the Three Bears.** *It is made from a combination of padded appliqué and free-standing forms. Such a design could be adapted to make a quilt.*
(Mouse Katz)

5

6

such as polyester satin and slipper satin, with interfacing sandwiched between. Machine-outline leaf shapes using a close zigzag stitch, and then cut out each leaf from the sandwich of fabric.
5 *Sew a central vein of gold cord down the middle of each leaf. Make the branches from tubes of background fabric, sewing into place as a network of branches across the top of the frame. Attach the leaves to the branches by their corners.*
6 *To make Goldilocks, cut a head and a small slug shape from calico and fill with wadding. Sew the head to the body and tuck the body under the blanket. Edge the blanket in crossway strip (bias binding), then hand-sew it down. Finally, make Goldilocks' hair: braid wool and metallic gold thread and sew it onto her head and over the frame.*

figures

Three-dimensional appliquéd sculpture became popular in the 1970s when artists who had previously worked in hard materials began to produce humorous pieces of work in soft fabrics, so that objects that were organically hard became soft, such as telephones, planes and typewriters. An exact pattern of the shape of the object would be cut from calico and then details would be added using applied fabrics. During the 1980s in both the United States and Australia, appliqué using knitted cotton jersey fabric to cover wadding or cotton became a popular method of creating caricatures of well-known people.

Today, artists create appliqué sculptures that are serious, rather than humorous, in intent. The work of Agnes Chevalier and Beverleigh Jones, shown here, share a theatricality in form, but they are very different in appearance.

Jones creates small, exquisite dolls, too beautiful and too delicate to be given to a child. They are inspired by her background in theatrical design. Shakespearian imagery, historic ballet costumes, *commedia dell'arte* characters and fashion designs by Erté all provide inspiration for this artist. Each doll is created individually, using many textile techniques, including appliqué. Many of the materials are hand-painted, dyed or printed before being appliquéd into place. Agnes Chevalier's work is more dream-like than Jones's. Her compositions are often surrounded by a soft appliquéd frame, from which figures languish as if draped in cobwebs.

Left: Rich swathes contrast with the simple figure fabric. (Agnes Chevalier)

Above: This doll is made from appliquéd, painted and dyed fabrics. (Beverleigh Jones)

frames

Appliquéd fabric frames have been produced commercially for the last 25 years, particularly in America, where great emphasis has been placed on co-ordinating furnishings. One of the most popular styles of appliqué frame is for the nursery, where simple, bold shapes in primary colours are easily transformed into appliqués. Alice in Wonderland stepping into a mirror is one of the more successful appliqué frame designs that I have seen. The back view of an appliquéd Alice covers part of the mirror by stepping into it, while characters such as the Queen of Hearts, the Cheshire Cat, and Tweedledee and Tweedledum are all appliquéd onto the frame.

A frame that is made from the fabrics which predominate in a particular room will help create a particular mood. Although made in a different way from her pillows, cushions or throws, Lorna Moffat's frames use the same colours and patterns to conjure up a rich, lush atmosphere.

When designing your own frames it is worth looking at examples made in different materials, such as carved wood or moulded plaster, for inspiration; consider the work of the Baroque sculptor Grinling Gibbons, who carved limewood festoons of flowers, leaves and fruit. Using similar methods to Lindsay Ellis (see page 136) you could create a Grinling-Gibbons-style frame in appliqué.

As well as creating three-dimensional shapes such as shells, flowers and fruit yourself, you can use bought fabric flowers, plaster fruit and real feathers to embellish your appliqué frames.

*Right and left: Silk and velvet reverse appliqué, machine stitched and cut away, is mounted onto a wooden frame and treated with a hardener. Enamel paint highlights the surround.
(Lorna Moffat)*

*Below: This elaborate shell frame is discussed overleaf.
(Lindsay Ellis)*

The mirror frame pictured here is inspired by Italian Renaissance gardens, in particular what was known as the grotto – an elaborate, glistening facade which had water tumbling over rocks and shells, highlighted with semi-precious stones. The artist first made sketches of grottoes and detailed drawings of shells, working in pencil, graphite powder and gold paint. As well as the reference drawings, she worked from real shells to help her with form when creating three-dimensional shapes. Her shell and starfish drawings are highly detailed and supplemented with colour references and sample swatches of fabrics.

The work consists of many techniques, including rucheing, padding, moulding, cutting and forming, machine embroidery and bead-work. The process of building layers of thread in a random fashion allows

How to make a shell mirror frame

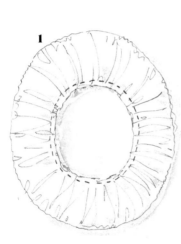

Equipment and materials

- Foam-covered board
- Wadding
- Scrim
- Mirror
- Sewing-machine with embroidery function
- Dressmaking scissors
- Craft knife
- Tacking thread
- Milliner's wire
- Metallic fabric paints

- Fabrics including calico and yard/metre lengths of silks and satins
- Tissue lamé
- Beads
- Crystals
- Sequins
- Needles
- Pins
- Sewing-machine needles
- Glue
- Sewing thread

1 Cut out the final shape of the mirror from foam-covered board and pad the edge of this backing with polyester wadding, leaving the middle free for the mirror. Cover the wadding in scrim and stitch in place with large basting stitches. Stick the mirror in position. The edges of the backing should surround, and be considerably deeper than, the mirror.
2 To make the bases for the shells, cut calico rectangles and stitch across these rectangles in rows, using small, neat running stitches. Gather and draw up the rows to different degrees so that the bottom edge is shorter than the top.

For the tops of the shells cut out rough shapes from scraps of fabrics such as velvet, silk, satin and tissue lamé (cut 4-5 pieces for each shell). Layer these on top of one another from light tones to dark to create the contour of the shell. Machine stitch in rows across the fabric sandwich using running stitch.
3 Trim the edges of the shape you have made so that it forms a three-dimensional oyster shell. Machine embroider the surface of the shell to add thickness. Glue or sew each shell top to its base and then attach the finished shells to the mirror surround.

To make the conch and snail shells, follow the method outlined in Step 2 but instead of cutting a shell shape, work in rectangular segments. Once you have attached the top of each appliquéd fabric segment to its base, piece three or four segments

you to "paint" with the thread by blending colours and textures. When using metallic thread, it is worth noting that it is less likely to break if it is threaded onto the bobbin spool. This reduces the tension on the metallic thread that would be created by threading it through the machine needle. However, it means that you then need to machine-stitch onto the reverse side of the fabric.

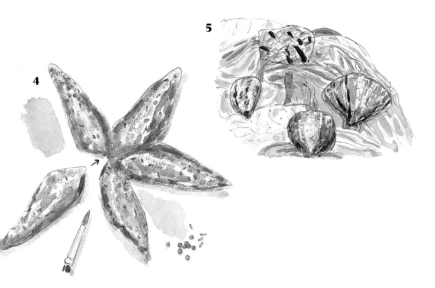

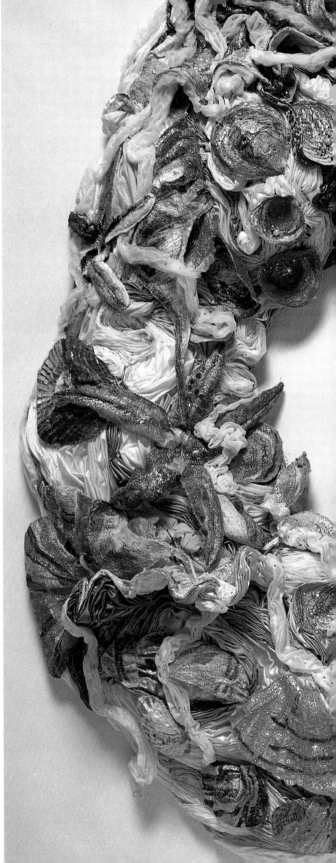

together, twisting them to form spirals. Stitch the segments together using a small overcast stitch.

4 *To make the starfish, follow the layering method you used for the tops of the shells. Cut out long oblongs, tapering the "feet" ends. Use appliquéd layers of fabric for the tops of each leg and plain satin for the underside. Seam the sides of each leg, leaving the top of the leg open. Pad each leg with polyester wadding and then stitch them all together to form a star shape. Appliqué and embroider over the joins. Finally, decorate the starfish with metallic fabric paints and a scattering of sewn-on beads. Finish by hand-sewing little circles of stitches all over the surface of the starfish.*

5 *Ruche extra-lightweight silk and stitch it across and around the shells to create a waterfall effect. Fix each starfish into the silk background to give the impression of water running over them. Decorate the ruched silk by sewing on crystal drops.*

6 *To make the large clam shells at the top of the mirror, cut seven or eight large, fan-shaped segments from metallic tissue, lamé and similar shiny fabrics. Make up the tops and bases using the same methods as the other shells (see Steps 2 and 3), but sew wire onto the back of the finished clam shell sandwich to create ribs and to help bend the shell into its final shape. Finally, sew each clam shell into position on the frame.*

directory of artists and suppliers

A

American Country Collection
Limited
28 Baker Street
Weybridge
Surrey KT13 8AU

Jeanette Appleton
4 Almshoebury Cottages
Near St. Ippolyts
Hitchin
Herts SG4 7NS
(0462) 457669

Kerry Avis
c/o M.V. Sabine
Dreadnorth Warf
Thames Street
Greenwich SE10 9BY
(0836) 268 068

B

Caroline Banks
307 Upland Road
London SE22 ODL
(081) 693 7385

Imogen Bittner
84 route de l'Odet
29950 Gouesnach
France
(010) 3398546932

Vanessa Blackmore
Blackwell Cottage
Glun
Craven Arms
Shropshire

Jilli Blackwood
8 Cleveden Crescent
Glasgow
G12 0PB

Janet Bolton
40 Aislible Road
Lee Green
London
SE12 8QQ

Hazel Bruce
Flat 14
20-22 Whalley Road
Whalley Range
Manchester
M16 8AB

C

Agnes Chevalier
10 Coverdale Road
London W12 8JL

Gillian Clarke
173 Melton Road
West Bridgford
Nottingham NG2 6JL

Amanda J Clayton
24 School Road
Wombourne
West Midlands WV5 9ED

Judy Clayton
64 Queens Road
Farnborough
Hampshire GU14 6DX

Brenda Conner
13 Sevenoaks Avenue
Heaton Moor
Stockport SK4 4AP

D

Jan Davies
Old Court Gallery
Symonds Yat West
Herefordshire HQ9 6DA

Veronica Double
52 Selcroft Road
Purley
Surrey CR8 1AS

E

Lindsay Ellis
141 Underhill Road
London SE22

F

Karen Fleming
29 Hillsborough Parade
Belfast BT6 9DU

Sandra Francis
107 Head Street
Halstead
Essex CO9 2AZ

G

General Trading Company
144 Sloane Street
London SW1X 9BL
(071) 730 0411

Stephanie Gilbert
'Farwood'
Richmond Road
Bowdon, Altrincham
Cheshire WA14 2TT

Sandra Grant
12 Neville Drive
Thatcham
Berkshire RG13 4PY

H

Jean Haig
108 Higher Lane
Lymm
Cheshire WA13 0BY

Gillian Horn
Shavards Farm
Meonstoke
Southampton
Hampshire SO3 1NR

Karen Howse
11 Compton Drive
Maidenhead
Berkshire SL6 5JS

Paul Hughes
Antique & Ancient Textiles
3A Pembridge Square
London W2

J

Susan Jenkins
Museum Quilts
3rd Floor
254-258 Goswell Road
London EC1V 7EB

Claire Johnson
135 Beach Road
Hartford
Northwich
Cheshire CW8 3AD

Beverleigh Jones
397 Manchester QY
Bury
Lancashire BL9 9QU

Jen Jones Antiques
Pontbrendu
Llanybydder
Dyfed
Wales SA40 9UJ

K

Mouse Katz
6 Strathmore Gardens
London W8

Berjouhie Keleshian
c/o 47 Clapham High Street
London SW4 7TL

Susan Kennewell
20A Lansdowne Street
Hove,
East Sussex
BN3 1FQ

Sandi Kiehlman
73 Robertson Street
Glasgow G2 8QD

Sarah King
Waterside Studios
Archers Wharf
99 Rotherhithe Street
London SE16 4NF

L

Liberty Retail Limited
Regent Street
London W1R 6AH

Dot Linton
53D Fernlea Road
London SW12

M

Jane McArthur
57 Comly Bank Avenue
Edinburgh EH4 1ET
(031) 343 2025

Rosemary McCloughlin
3 Merton Road
Rathmines
Dublin 6
Eire

Faith Manzira
6 Wheatley Park Road
Bentley Doncaster
S. Yorkshire DN5 0JN

Grace Meijer
Stowe Cottage
Balchins Lane
Westcott
Surrey RH4 3L12

Corliss Miller
86 St Michaels Avenue
Yeovil,
Somerset
BA21 4LG

Lorna Moffat
38 Canon Woods Way
Kennington
Ashford
Kent TN24 9QY

Liz Mundle
Limited Edition Embroidery
73 Badminton Road
London SW12 8BL

N

Neal Street East
7 Neal Street
Covent Garden
London WC2H 9PU

O

Oxfam Trading
P.O. Box 182
274 Banbury Road
Oxford
OX2 7D2

P

Dawn Pavitt
12 Napier Court
Gafle Close
Balfic Wharf
Bristol
BS1 6XY

Jane Prichett
3 Abbeylane
Aslockton
Nottingham
NG13 99E

Herta Puls
Beverley
Magor Road
Langstone
Newport
Gwent NP6 2JX

R

Jo Ratcliffe
4 Ribblesdale Place
Preston
Lancs PR1 3NA

S

Maureen Sawyer
Southlands
12 Sandy Lane
Stretford
Manchester
Lancs M32 9DA

T

Linda Tudor
Keston Cottage
Downs Lane
Leatherhead
Surrey KT22 8JJ

V

Rose Verney
16 Hardwick Street
Newnham
Cambridge CB3 9JA

W

Juliet Walker
23 Golden Crescent
Everton
Lymington
Hampshire SO41 0LN

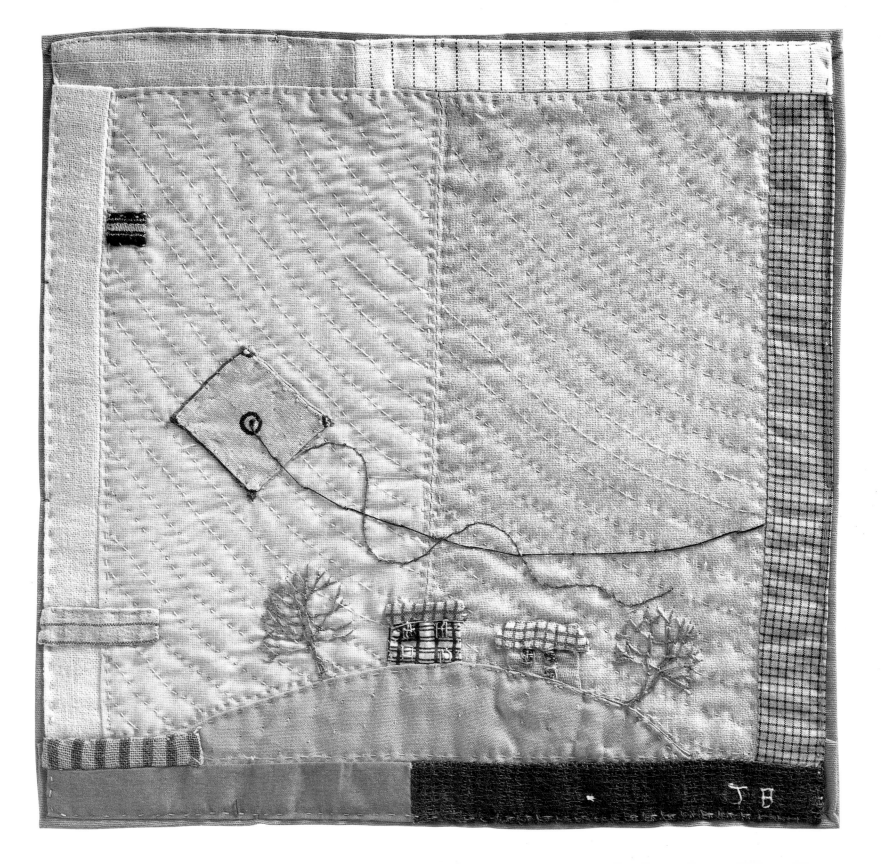

The pieces in this book were made (or collected) and kindly loaned by the following:

P1	Linda Tudor
P2-3	Susan Kennewell
P6	Liz Mundle
P9	Susan Jenkins, Jen Jones and Ann Civardi
P11	Anne Scampton
P12	Susan Jenkins
P14	Oxfam Trading
P15	Victoria Davenport
P16&17	Neal Street East
P19	General Trading Company
P20&21	Paul Hughes
P22	Faith Manzira
P23	Sandra Francis
P25	Maureen Sawyer
P29	Jeanette Appleton
P30	Susan Kennewell
P31	Susan Kennewell
P32	Rose Verney
P33	Dawn Pavitt
P34	Linda Tudor

P35	Stephanie Gilbert
P37	Berjouhie Keleshian
P38	Stephanie Gilbert
P39	Gillian Horn
P41	Stephanie Gilbert
P42	Amanda Clayton
P43	Jane Prichett
P44	Rosemary McCloughlin
P45	Jo Ratcliffe
P46-47	Lorna Moffat
P48	Lorna Moffat
P50	Janet Bolton
P51	Janet Bolton
P52-53	Janet Bolton
P54	Jane McArthur
P55	Jane Prichett
P56-57	Hazel Bruce
P59	Karen Howse
P60&61	Brenda Conner
P62-63	Sarah King
P65	Sarah King
P66	Maureen Sawyer
P67	Caroline Banks
P68-69	Sarah King
P70&71	Caroline Banks

P74	Jean Haig
P75	Amanda Clayton
P76&77	Amanda Clayton
P82	Gillian Clarke
P83	Gillian Clarke
P84-85	Dinah Prentice
P86	Dinah Prentice
P87	Jan Davies
P89	Grace Meijer
P90	Jilli Blackwood
P91	Jean Haig
P92-93	Sarah King
P95	Jeanette Appleton
P96	Imogen Bittner
P97	Karen Fleming
P98&99	Corliss Miller
P100&101	Vanessa Blackmore
P102	Sandi Kiehlman
P103	Maureen Sawyer
P104-105	Gillian Horn
P106	Vanessa Double
P107	Liz Mundle
P108-109	Kerry Avis
P110&111	Kerry Avis
P112	Sarah King

P113	Herta Puls
P115	Sarah King
P116-117	Jilli Blackwood
P120-121	Judy Clayton
P119	Sandra Francis
P123	Judy Clayton
P124	Claire Johnson (top), Linda Tudor (bottom)
P125	Juliet Walker
P128	Stephanie Gilbert
P129	Dot Linton
P131	Mouse Katz
P132	Agnes Chevalier
P133	Beverleigh Jones
P134	Lorna Moffat (left), Lindsay Ellis (right)
P135	Lorna Moffat
P137	Lindsay Ellis
P139	Lorna Moffat
P140	Janet Bolton
P143	Corliss Miller
P144	American Country Collection

index

author's acknowledgments

Page 1: A mixed-media appliqué that includes fabric, paper and paint. The Tibetan hand-painted paper background is combined with gold embroidered trellis and gold paint. The bottom edge of the piece is trimmed with hand-made silk tassels. Paper and fabric can be mixed if the item doesn't need washing. (Linda Tudor)

Pages 1-2: A detail of an appliqué hanging that incorporates machine embroidery and applied geometric shapes in bright colours on a dark background. (Susan Kennewell)

Page 139: Rich colour, fabrics and intricate patterns give a warm glow and depth to this work. (Lorna Moffat)

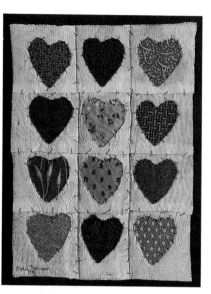

Page 140: A judicious use of natural and small print fabrics has produced this deceptively naive picture of flying kites. (Janet Bolton)

Page 143: Dyed, hand-painted and cut-away layers of fabrics have been used to create a delicate and effective abstract picture. (Corliss Miller)

Page 144 (left): A contemporary appliqué sampler using a repeated simple heart shape cut from old cotton fabrics. The edges are turned under and hand stitched onto unbleached calico. The calico squares are then roughly sewn together to form a complete picture. (The American Country Collection)

Thanks are due to my father who helped by proof-reading my original manuscript; Judith More, Larraine Lacey and Jacqui Small at Mitchell Beazley for their enthusiasm and encouragement; Kevin Hart for his wonderful drawings and Peter Marshall for his beautiful photographs.

Thanks also to Emma Gough at Oxfam Trading for information on folk applique; to Mr Noel-Hill at the American Country Collection Limited, 28 Baker Street, Weybridge, Surrey KT13 8AU, for the loan of quilts and a picture; to the National Patchwork Association, PO Box 300, Hethersett, Norwich, Norfolk NR9 3BB for their help in tracking down many of the contributors in the book; to Susan Jenkins at Museum Quilts (antique American quilts), 3rd Floor, 254-258 Goswell Road, London EC1V 7EB; to Jen Jones Antiques (Welsh quilts and blankets, small antiques) Pontbrendu, Llanybydder, Dyfed, Wales SA40 9UJ for the loan of quilts; and to Mr Turner at Westgate Patchworks, 2 Lifeboat Hill, St Ives, Cornwall TR26 1LE for the loan of Dawn Pavitt's quilt.